The Grand Staircase

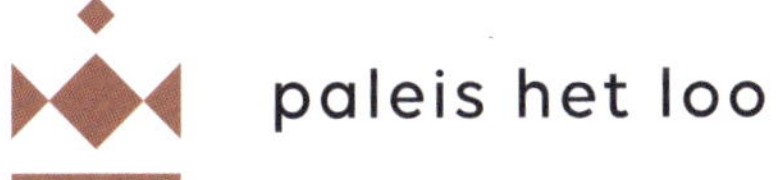

WAANDERS
UITGEVERS

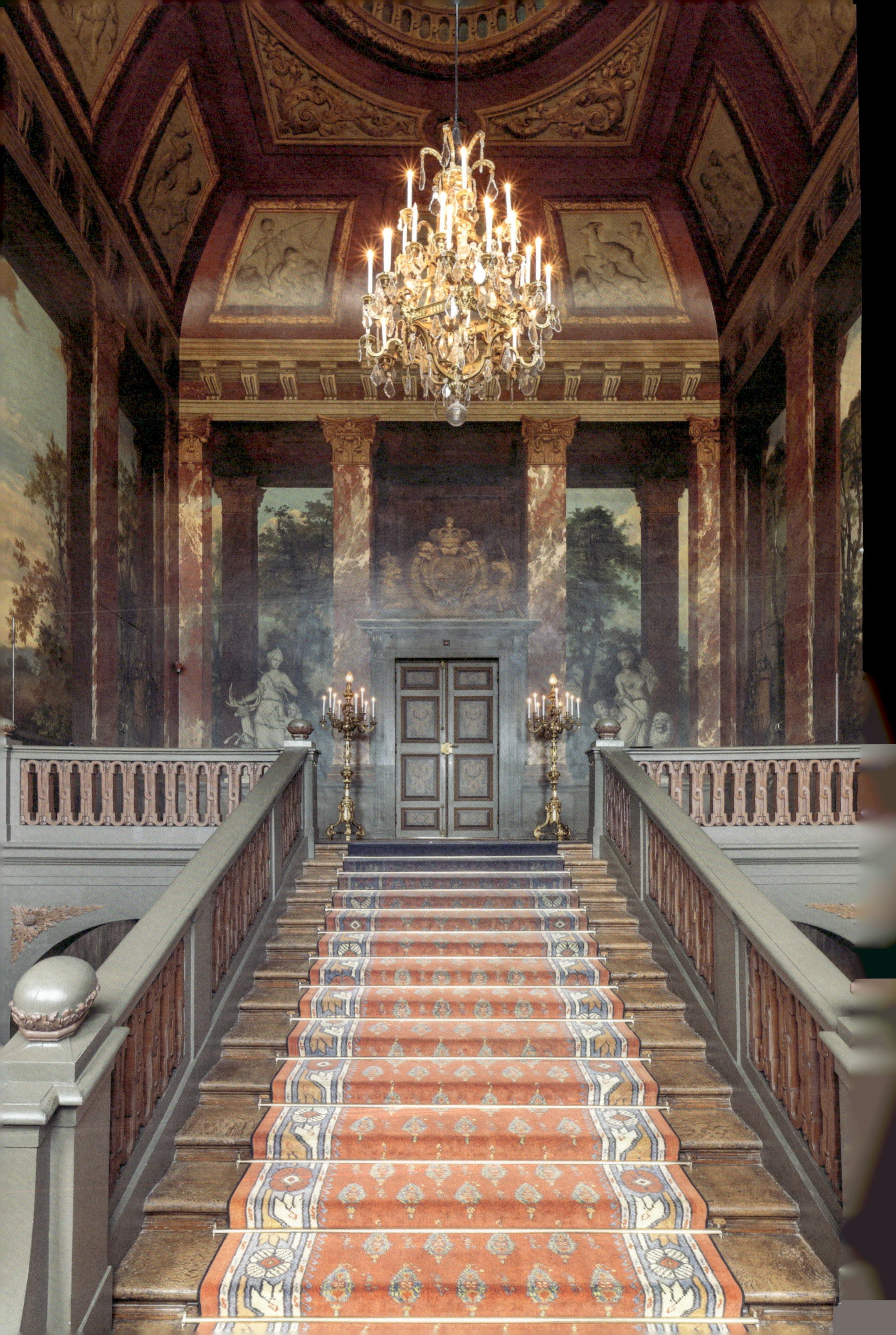

Contents

← The Grand Staircase leads to the Great Hall on the first floor.

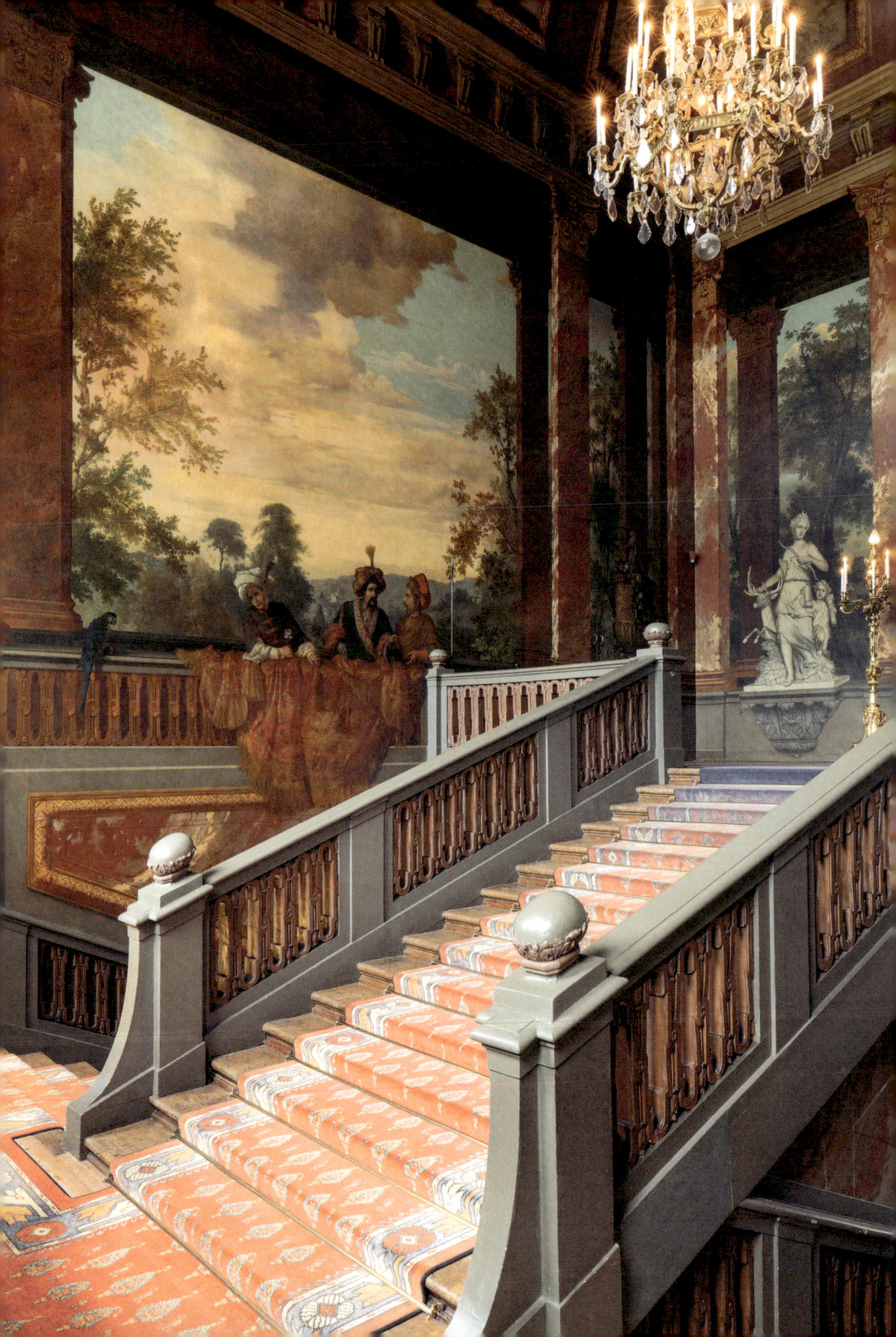

If Walls Could Talk

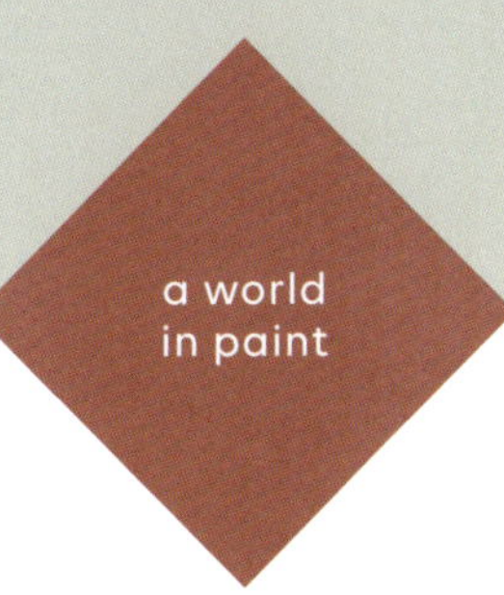

Visitors to Paleis Het Loo cannot possibly miss it: the Grand Staircase at the heart of the palace. The majestic staircase has 36 steps – old-fashioned shallow steps suitable for long skirts and close-fitting outfits. The staircase slows you down as you climb. A world in paint unfolds around you on the walls and ceiling. This is a staircase with a story.

The painting depicts a colonnade with glimpses of a distant vista. There are all kinds of details: a parrot, vases festooned with garlands of flowers, statues of goddesses. At the centre are seven figures – all men – leaning nonchalantly on the painted balustrades. They appear to be in conversation with each other, glancing with curiosity at the space below them. They are dressed in what looks like Ottoman attire. But who exactly they are and why they are depicted here remained a mystery for many years.

This monumental work has a long history. The original painting on the walls and ceiling was completed in circa 1692. Restoration work and changing taste completely changed the look of the staircase over the centuries. What visitors see today is a reconstruction from the early 20th century, based on old fragments and a 17th-century print depicting the original design.

← **The Grand Staircase at Paleis Het Loo.**

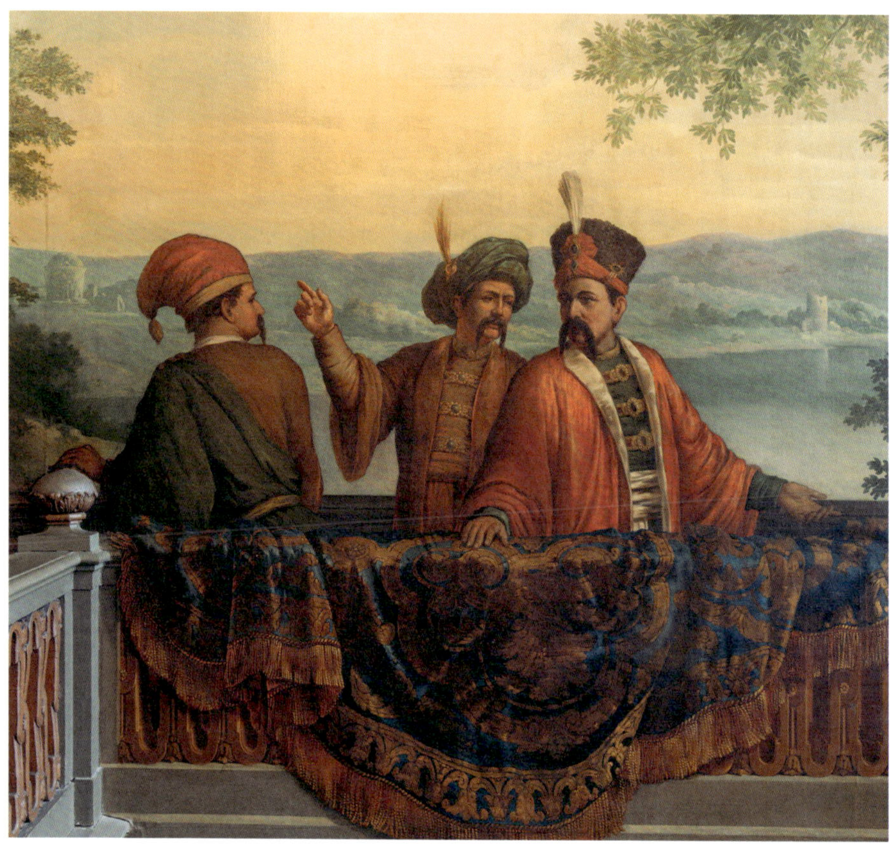

More than a century later, new research has revealed how we might interpret this artwork. The painting tells a remarkable story that takes us from the Veluwe region of the Netherlands to Versailles in France and on to Istanbul. It reflects the Dutch House of Orange's cultural and political ties with other royal courts and their involvement in world events around 1700. The painting is also part of the northern European tradition of monumental murals. Read on to discover the astonishing story of the Grand Staircase, and find out more about this unique piece of Dutch heritage.

↑ The men appear to be in conversation.

→ There are four vases with garlands dotted about the staircase.

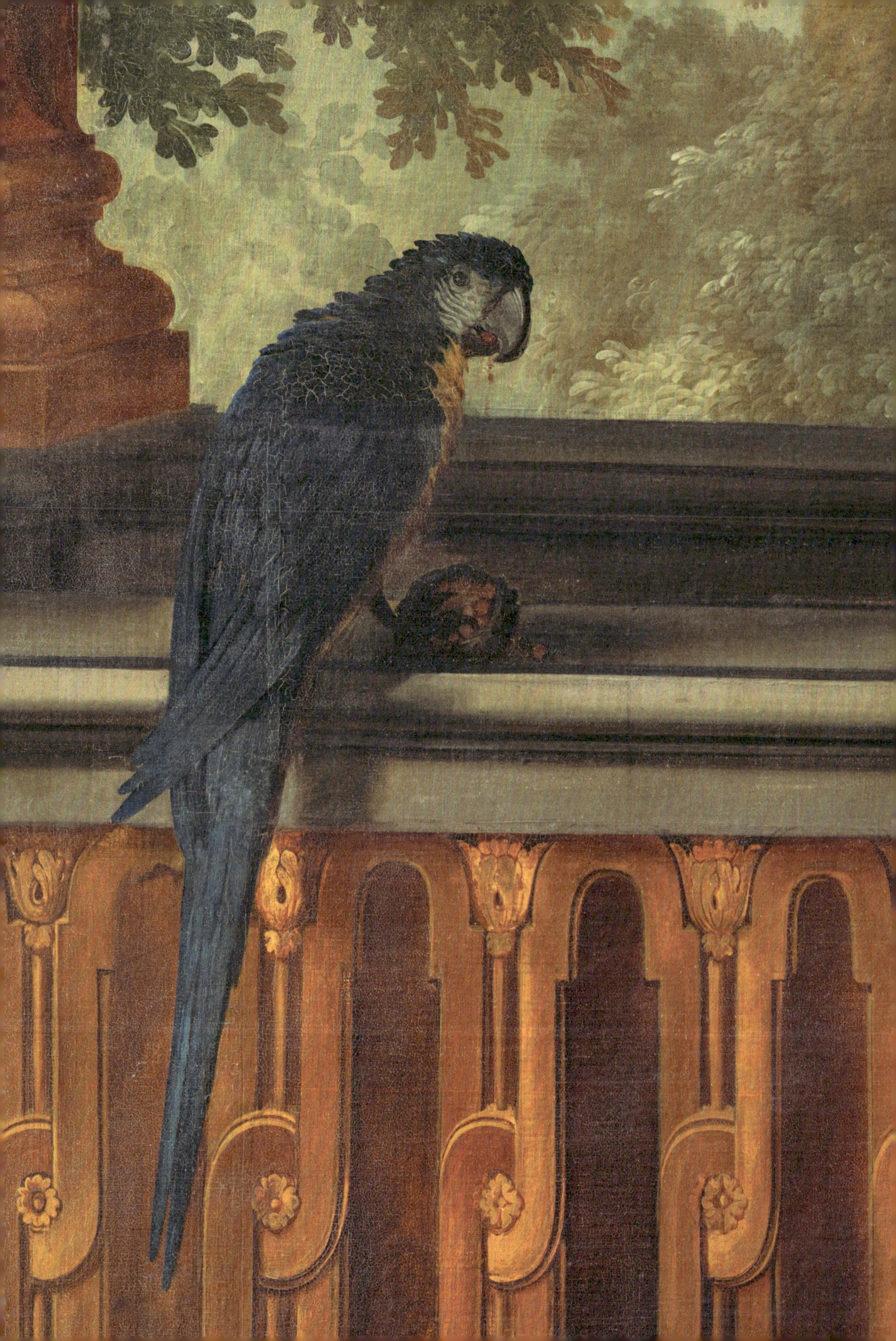

A Staircase with a View

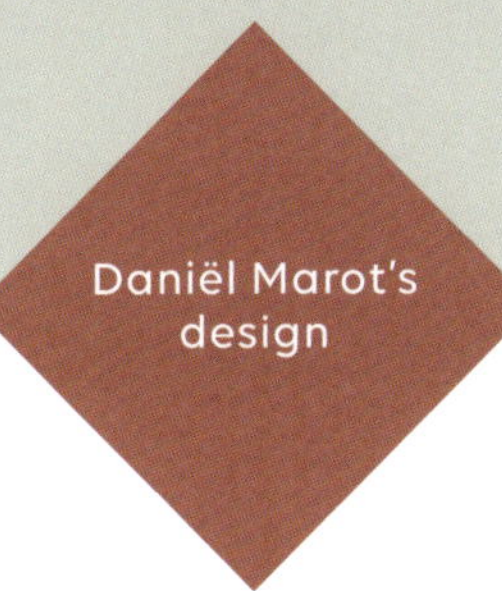

In 1684 Stadtholder Willem III (1650-1702) and his wife Princess Mary II Stuart (1662-1695) bought a medieval hunting lodge, Het Oude Loo, and the surrounding land. They had a new, more modern hunting lodge built beside the dated castle. Mary laid the first stone on 7 May 1685, and the building was completed just over a year later. This 'corps de logis' – French for 'main building' – is now the heart of Paleis Het Loo.

We do not know for certain who produced the original design for the palace. Architect Jacob Roman (1640-1716) was at any rate closely involved in the construction. The Grand Staircase was located just beyond the Entrance Hall, in the central axis of the structure. Willem III had instructed his ambassador in Paris to request designs from the prestigious Académie Royale d'Architecture. He received the drawings on 5 April 1685, a few weeks before construction commenced. Although Roman did not precisely follow the French designs, they do indicate that it was to France that Willem turned for inspiration. Baroque architecture was the fashionable style there at the time. Buildings were symmetrical, and built on a grand scale. The interiors had opulent decorations, featuring costly fabrics, marble and gold details. In the Dutch Republic, this exuberant style was toned down somewhat to produce the Dutch baroque as exemplified by Paleis Het Loo.

← A parrot seated on the balustrade watches as visitors come and go.

From hunting lodge to royal palace

Willem and Mary became King and Queen of England, Scotland and Ireland in February 1689, following the peaceful overthrow of the English King James II (1633–1701), Mary's father. Certain influential aristocrats invited Willem and Mary to accede to the throne in his place. To emphasise their new royal status, they had major extension work carried out on their palaces, starting in summer 1689. Hampton Court and Kensington Palace in London were extended, as was Paleis Het Loo, which would henceforth be used as a royal summer palace.

→ Mary II Stuart portrayed by Willem Wissing in circa 1686 (detail).

↗ King-Stadtholder Willem III portrayed by court painter Jan Hendrik Brandon in 1698 (detail).

↓ Today's Paleis Het Loo with the 'corps de logis', the original building, in the centre.

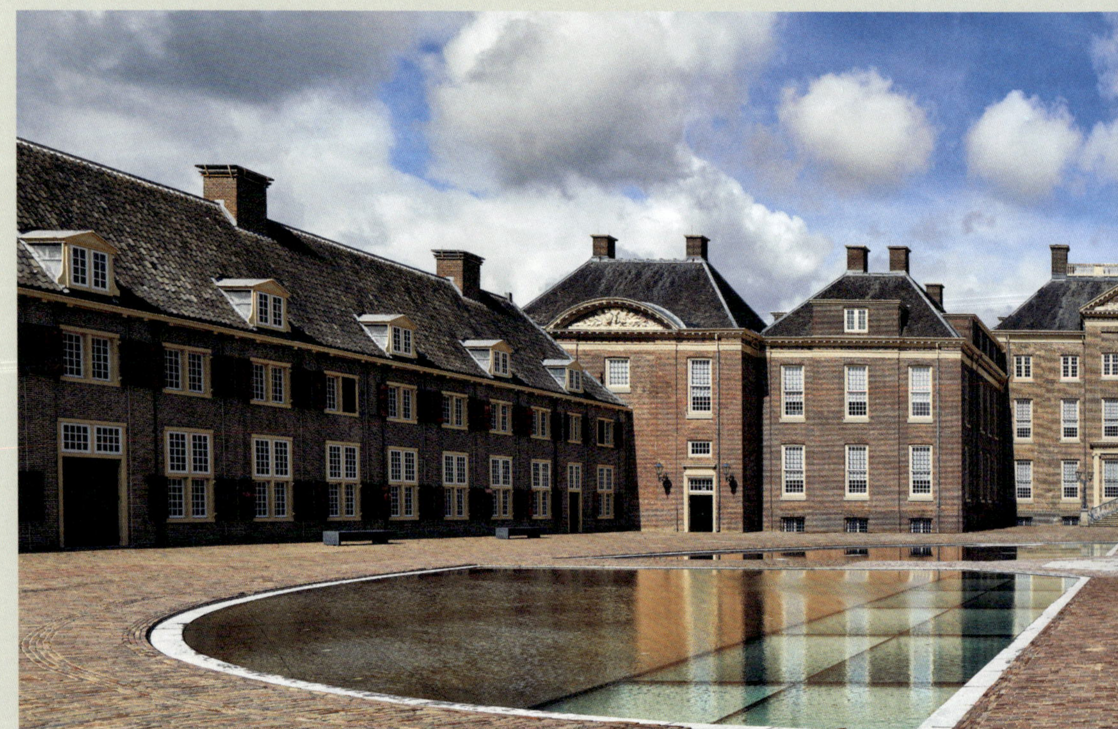

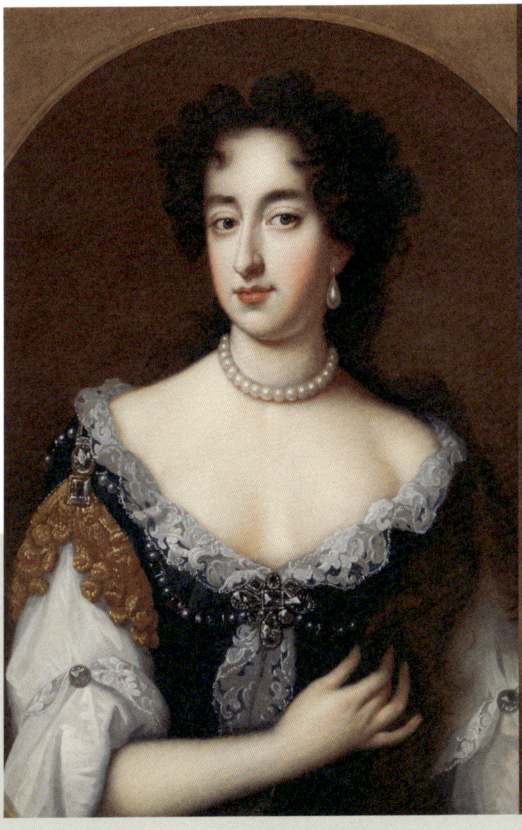

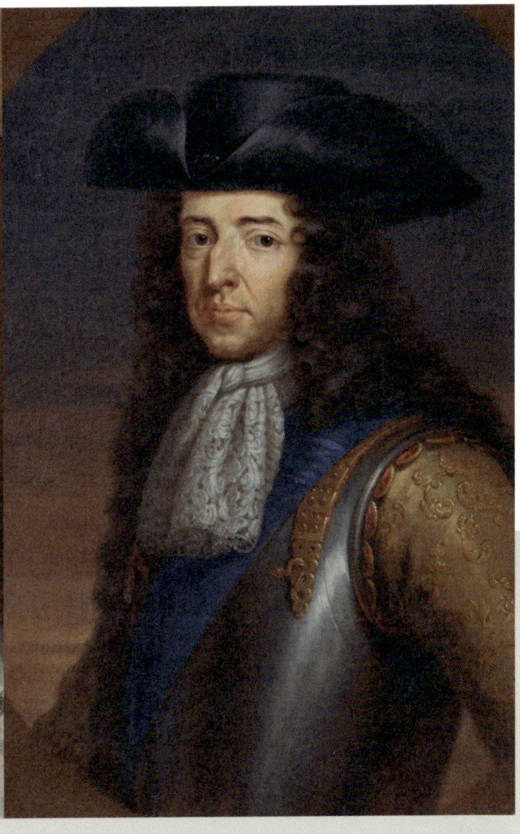

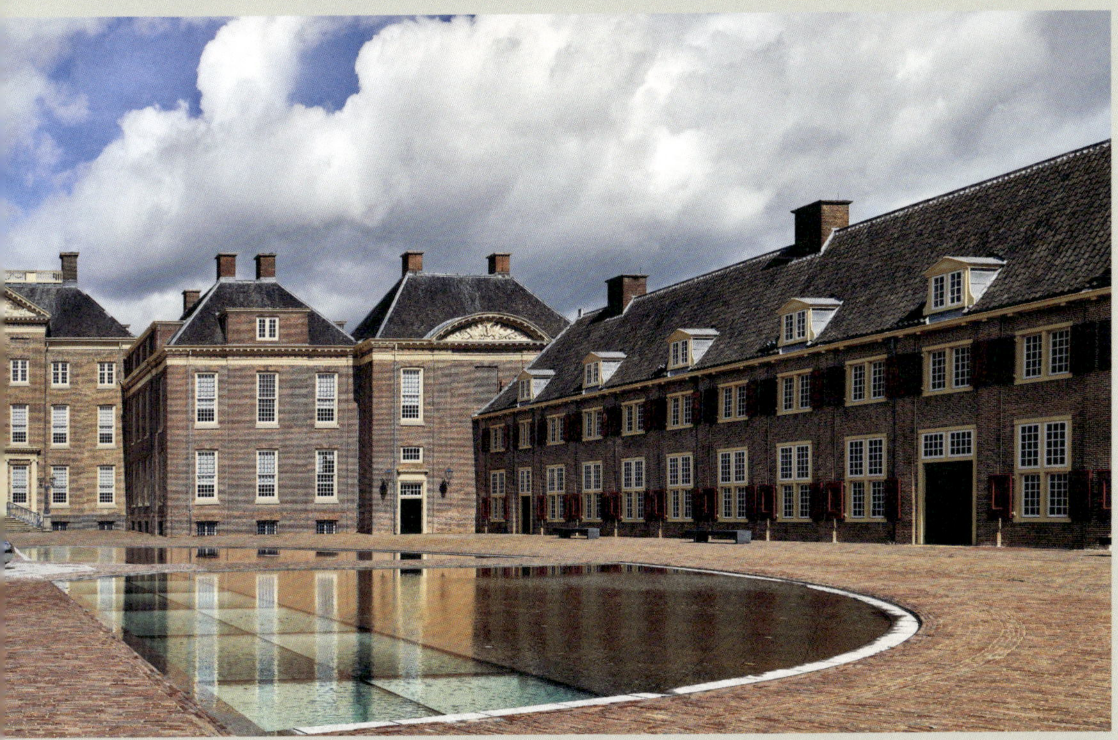

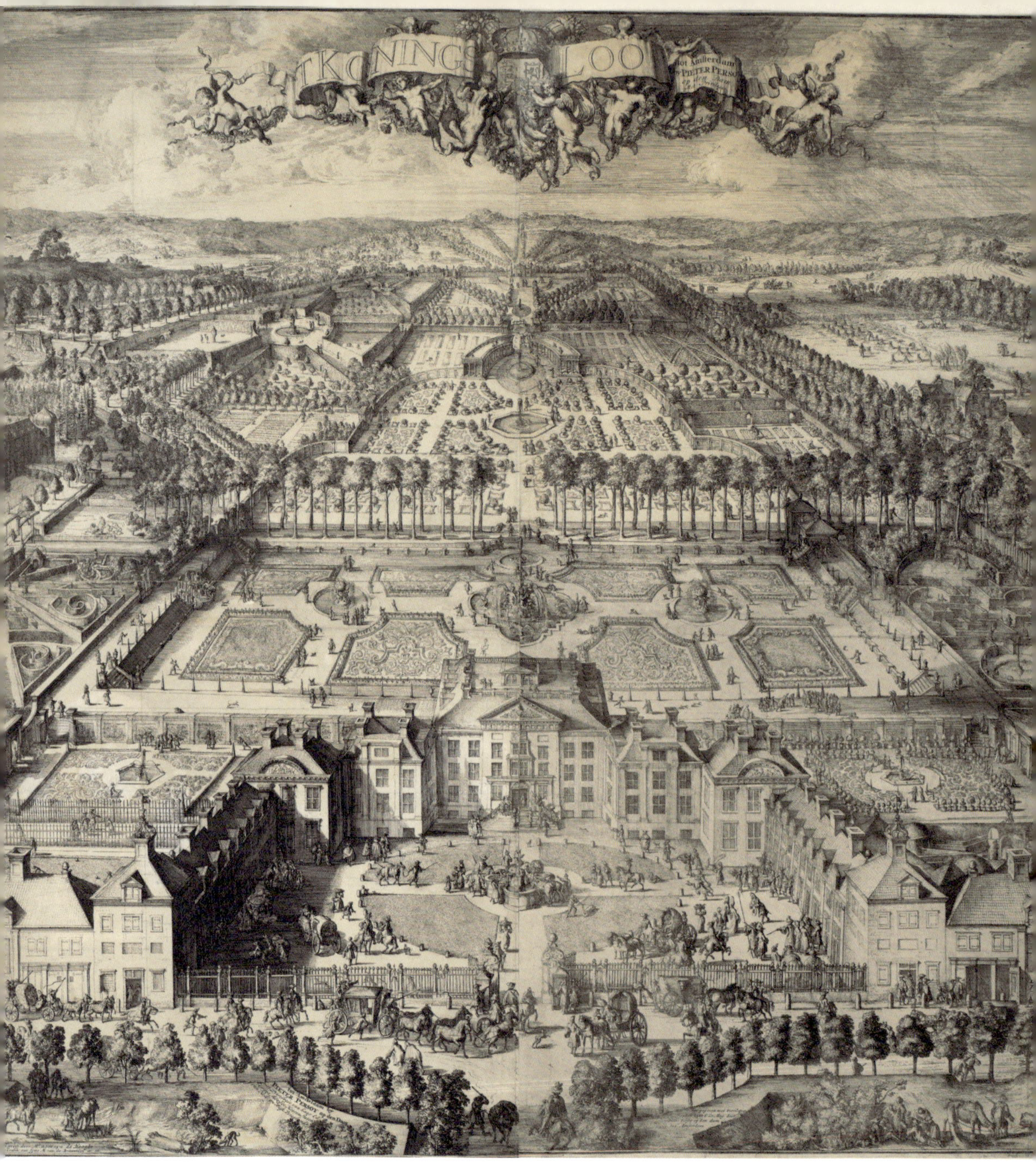

Romeyn de Hooghe produced this bird's-eye view in circa 1695, shortly after the palace was extended.

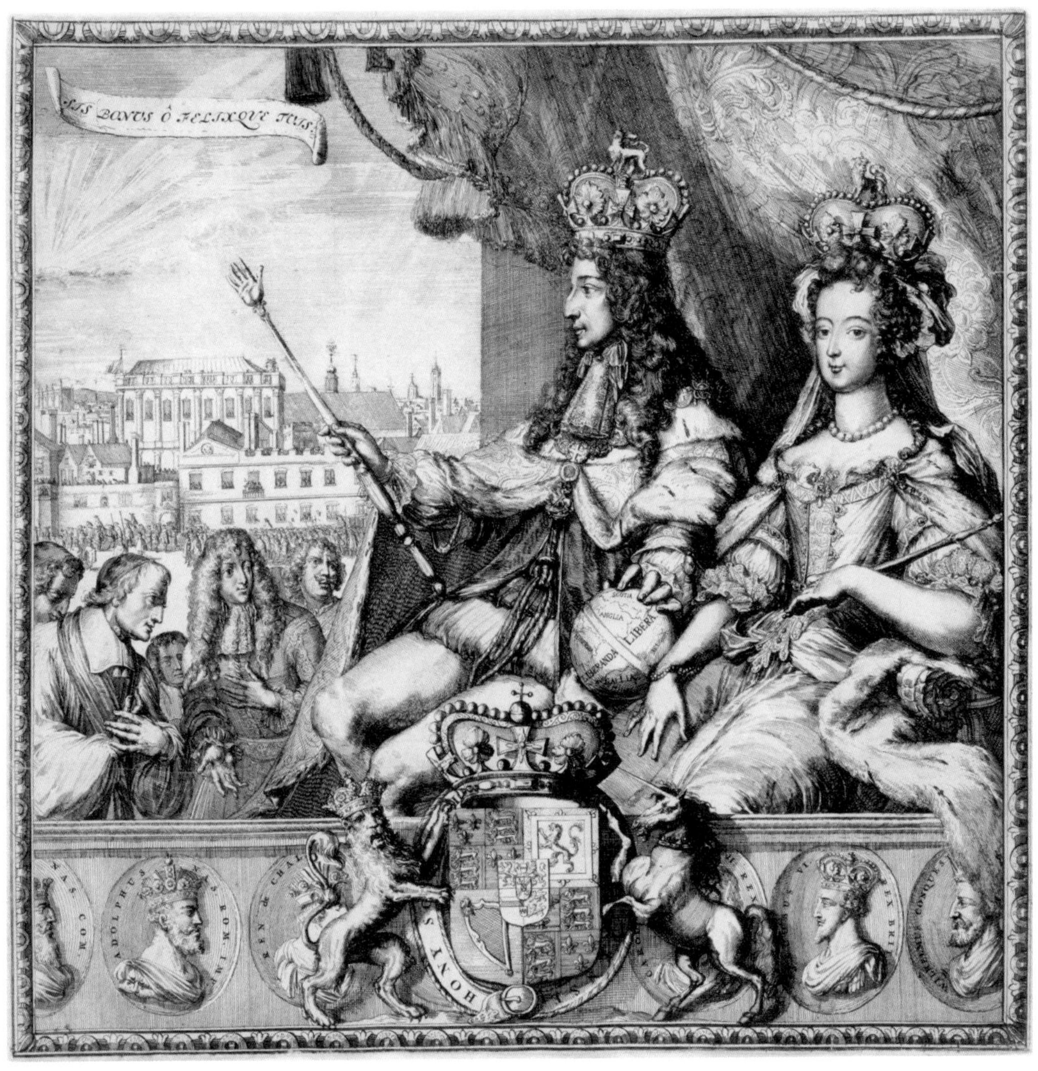

William and Mary as King and Queen of England, Scotland and Ireland in a print by Romeyn de Hooghe.

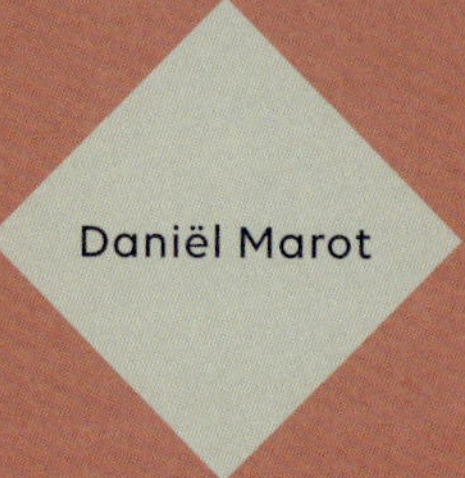

Daniël Marot

French artist Daniël Marot (1661-1752) played a key role in the decoration and furnishing of Paleis Het Loo. He was a Calvinist and had been forced to flee France with his family in 1685, when Protestants were persecuted after Louis XIV issued the Edict of Fontainebleau. Marot found a safe haven at the court of Willem III, who was happy to make use of his talent. He produced designs for Willem's palaces in both the Dutch Republic and England. Marot was responsible for a large portion of the interior of Paleis Het Loo. He also designed a lot of the furniture and many garden ornaments.

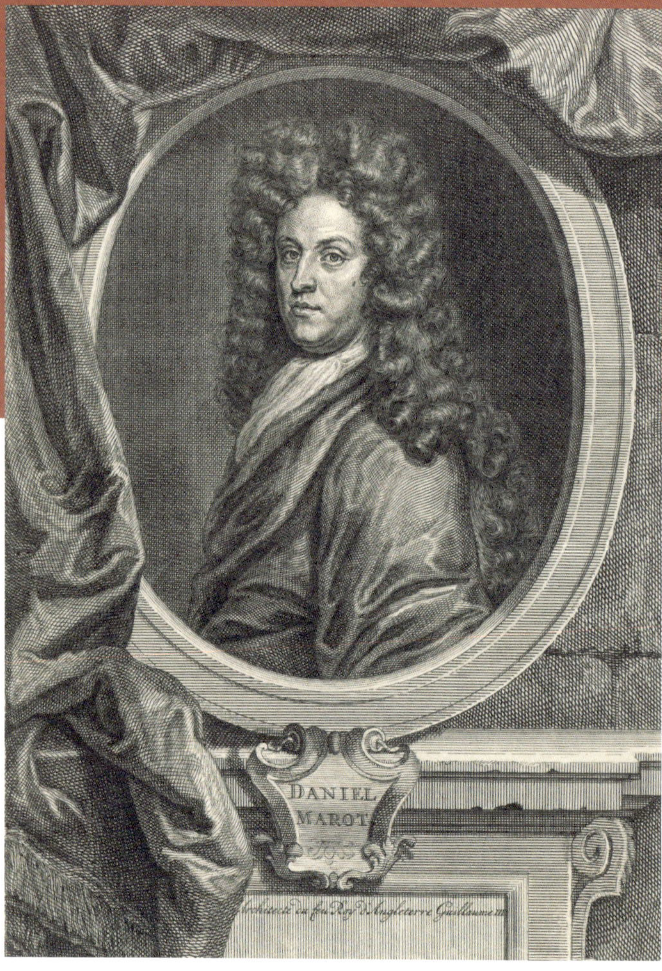

Daniël Marot, portrayed in an engraving by Jacob Gole.

Comprehensive design

The palace as we know it was created during the second phase of construction, from 1690 to 1694. Pavilions were added to the 'corps de logis' to connect it to the side wings, and the gardens were expanded. Between 1690 and 1693 the walls and ceiling of the Grand Staircase were decorated with a contiguous painting covering some 550 square metres, executed in oil on plaster. The design was by Daniël Marot.

For the east and west walls of the staircase Marot designed a colonnade with vaulting that continued onto the ceiling. The architectural painting creates an optical illusion, making the space appear higher than it is in reality. The columns and vaulting were painted directly on the walls in oil. Between the columns, men casually lean against the balustrades. On the east wall, a parrot sits beside them. On both walls, in the corners, there are two large garden vases with a garland of flowers draped over them. Beyond the balustrades, there are views of a distant landscape, seamlessly merging the interior and exterior.

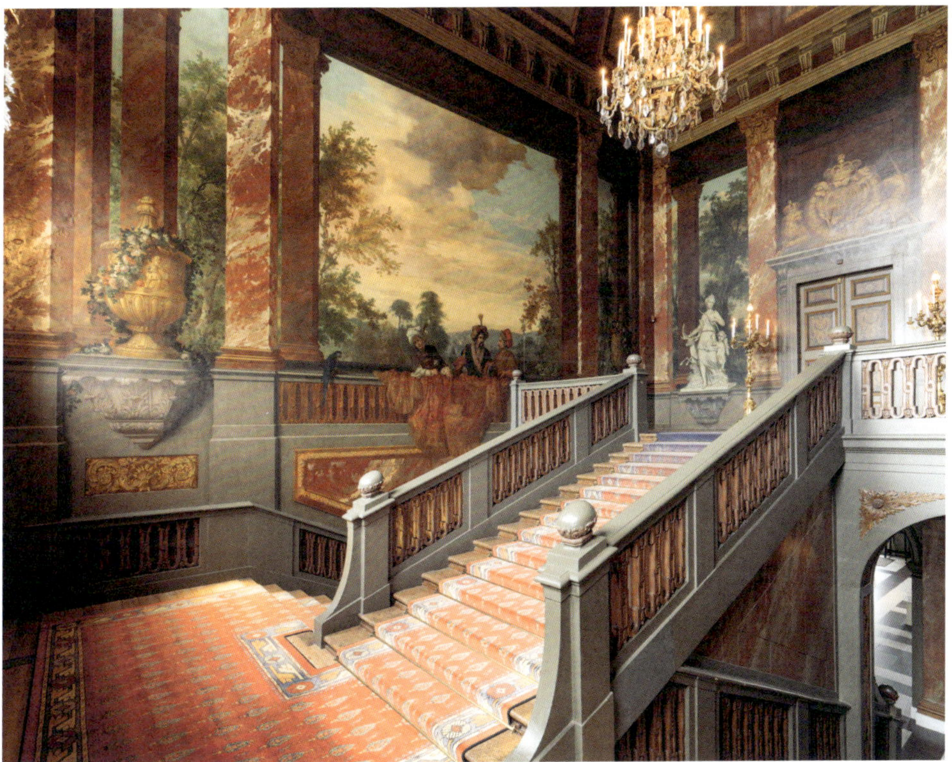

The painting on the east wall, seen from the first landing.

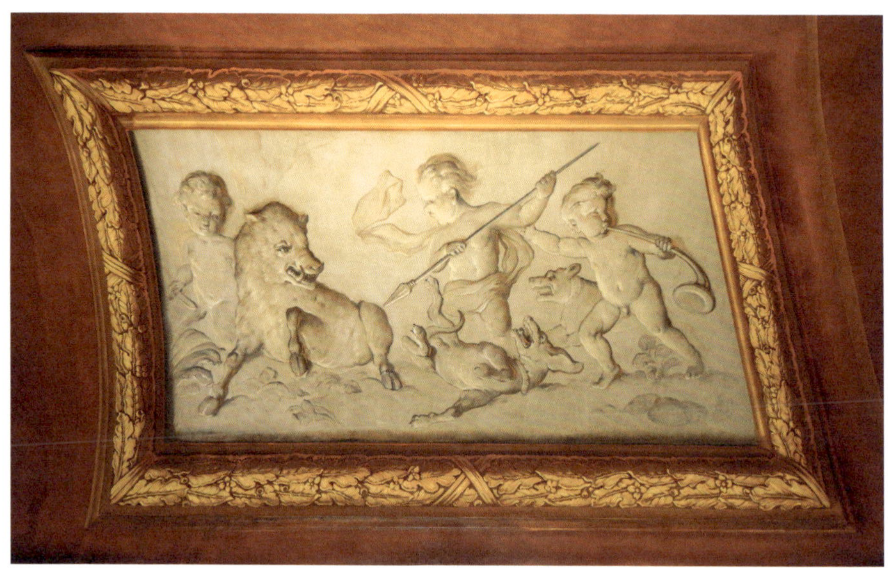

A painted 'oculus', a circular opening in the ceiling, gives the impression that we are looking straight at the sky. Reliefs are painted around it in grey tones. They depict small naked figures known as putti engaged in all kinds of hunting activities, referring to the palace's original function. King-Stadtholder Willem III loved hunting.

Once the mural was completed, Marot made an etching of the finished result. It is likely that he did not use the painting itself as a reference, but rather a design sketch that has since been lost. It reveals that many elements of the wall paintings at Paleis Het Loo also occur in other designs by Marot. Yet there are noticeable differences too, making the Grand Staircase unique within his body of work. The two groups of men in Ottoman-style attire on the east and west walls of the staircase are particulary striking. They differ from the mythological or allegorical figures that Marot tended to depict in interiors like this, as at Slot Zeist and Huis de Voorst. Lavishly painted staircases were popular towards the end of the 17th century, and were a showpiece that graced many stately homes in the Netherlands.

↑ **A painted relief showing a scene with putti hunting.**

→ **The painted ceiling above the staircase.**

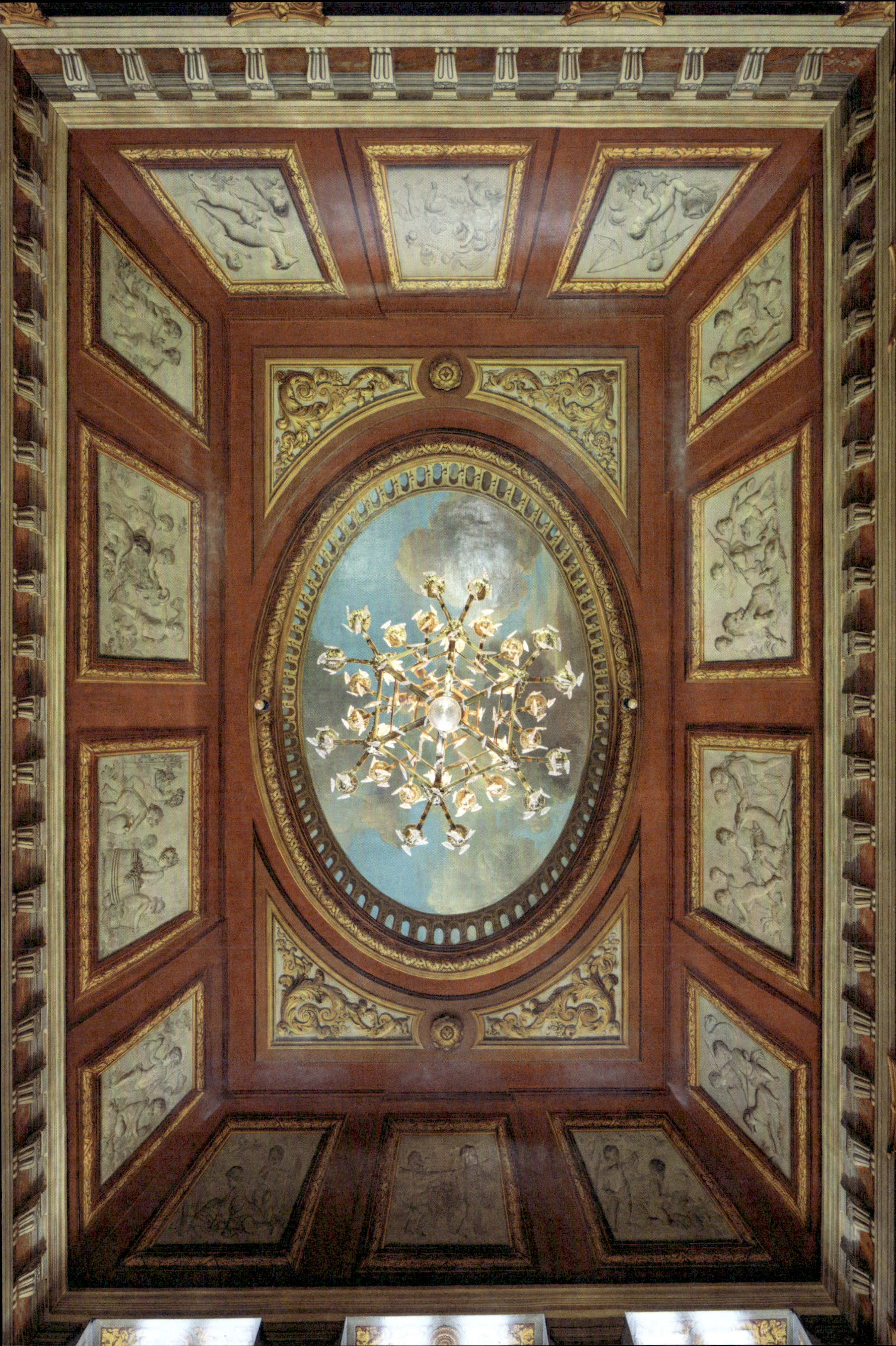

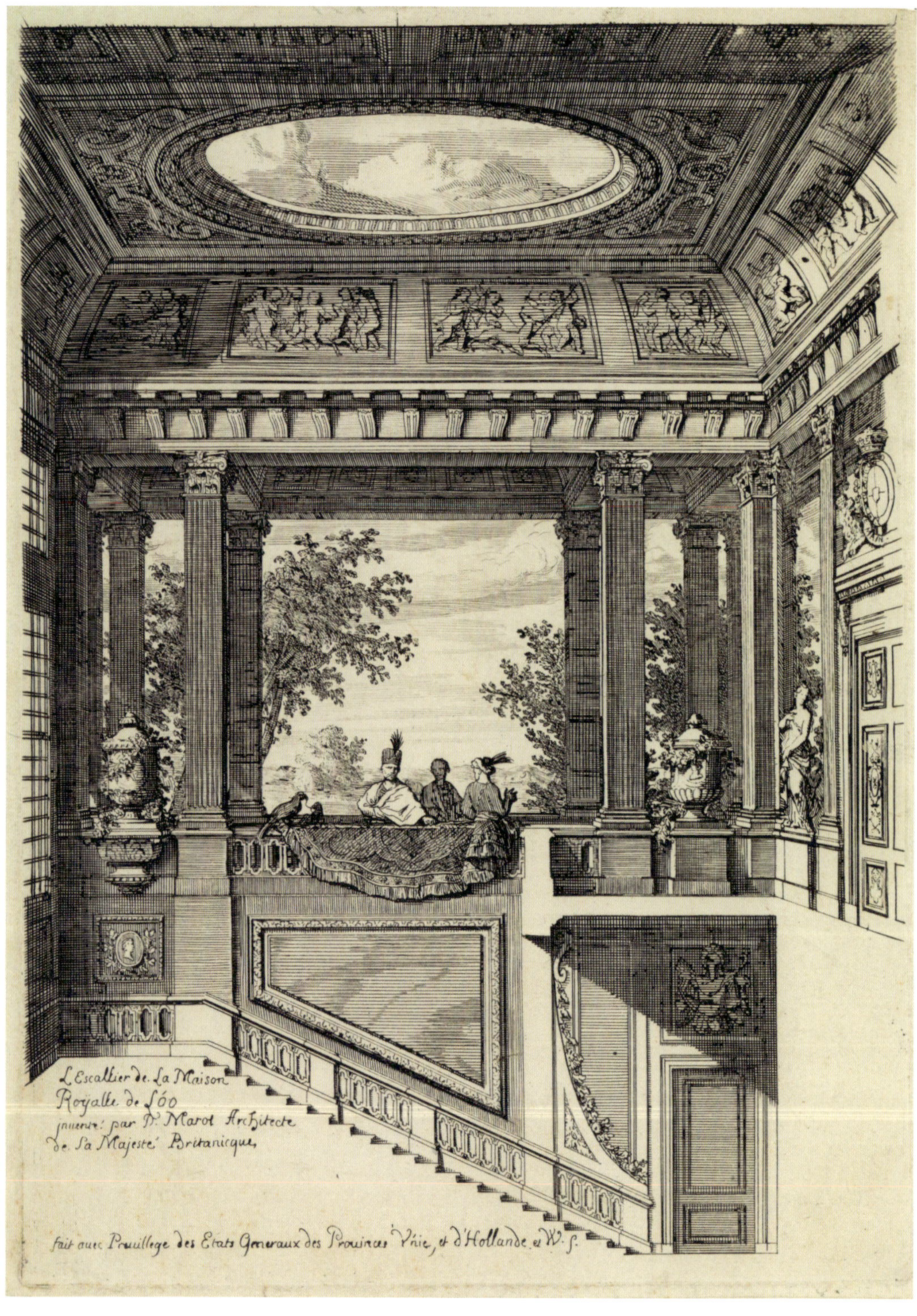

Marot produced this etching after the Grand Staircase was finished.

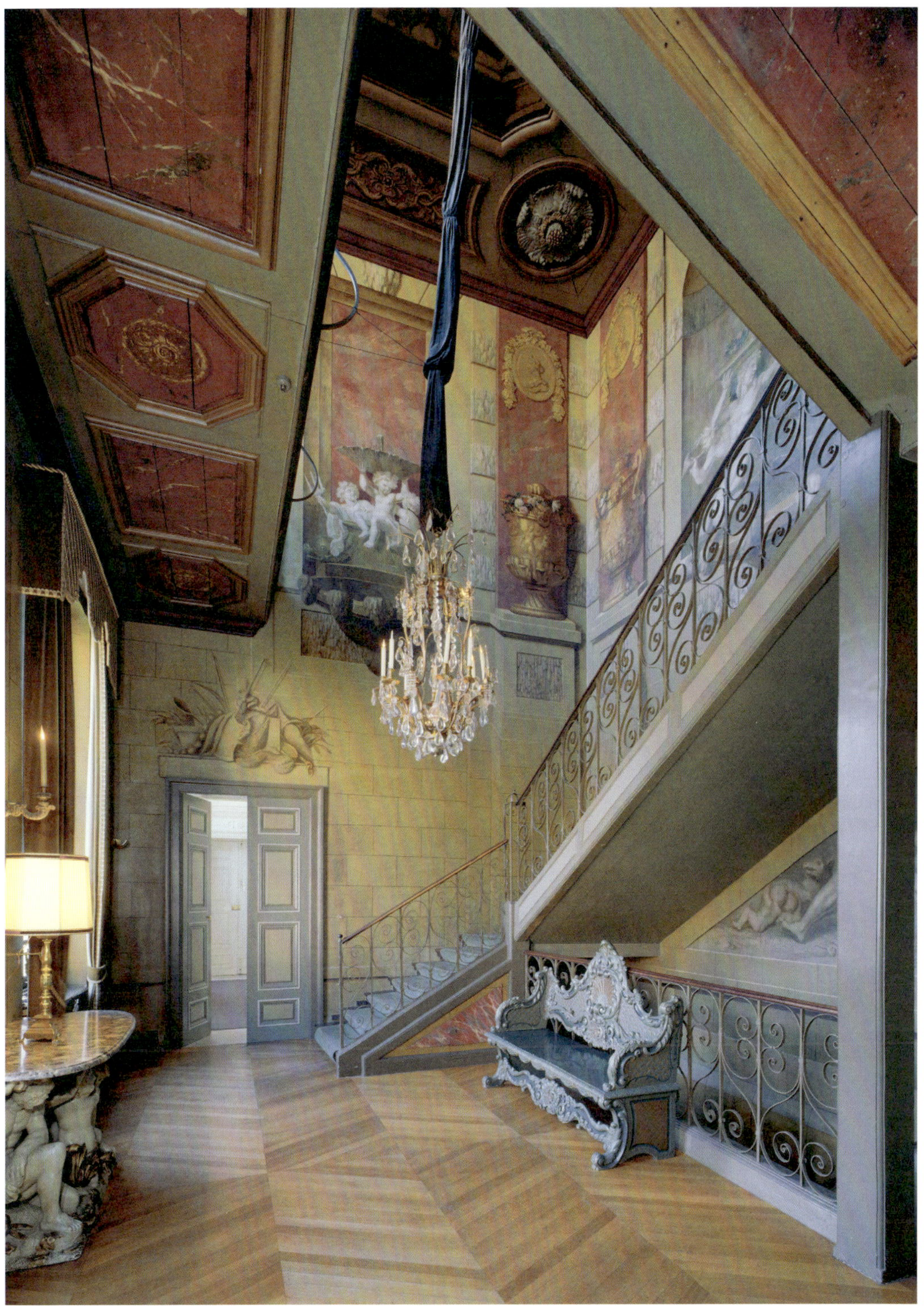

The staircase at Slot Zeist has mythological scenes on the walls.

Marot worked mainly as a designer, and no paintings actually executed by him have survived. His design for the Grand Staircase at Paleis Het Loo was largely executed by Robbert Duval (1649-1732), who had been Willem III's court painter since 1682. He was probably assisted by other artists, including Johannes Lotyn (1618-1695), who was responsible for the many flowers painted on the ceilings and above the doors in the palace.

A royal gesture

The staircase is the main link between the entrance hall, or vestibule, and the Great Hall on the first floor where Willem and Mary received important guests. In accordance with the tradition of Dutch court architecture, the stadtholder and his wife lived on this floor. Leading courtiers inhabited the ground floor. The staff lived and worked in the basement. Paleis Het Loo was no exception.

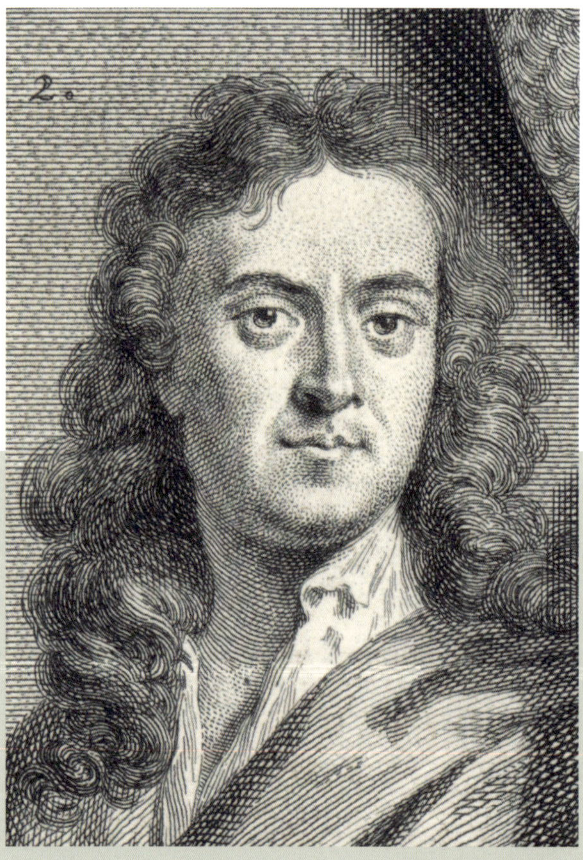

↑ In 1750 Pieter Tanjé etched this posthumous portrait of Robbert Duval based on a drawing by Aert Schouman, (detail).

→ Marot's design for the staircase at Huis de Voorst.

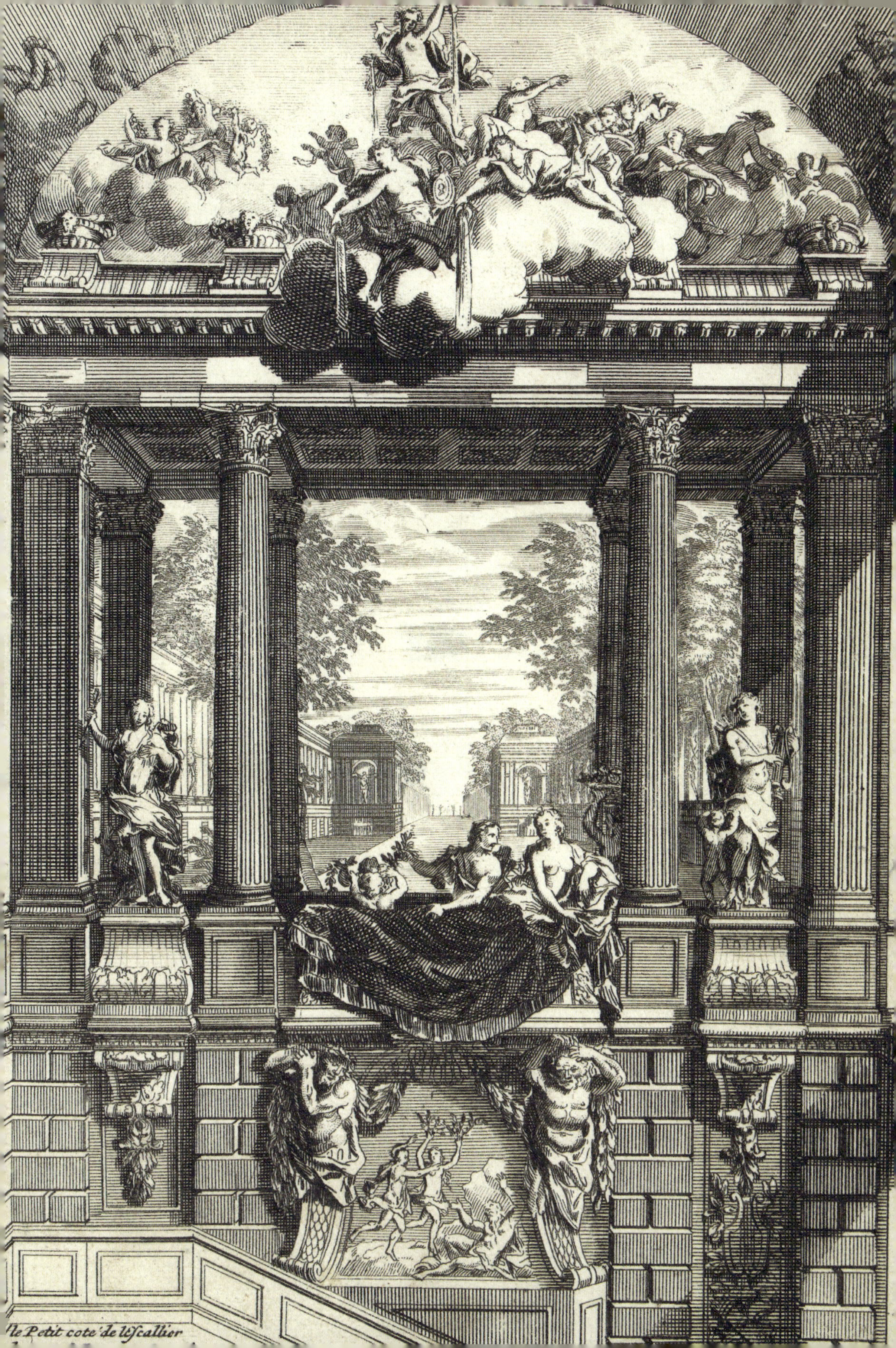
le Petit cote de l'Escallier

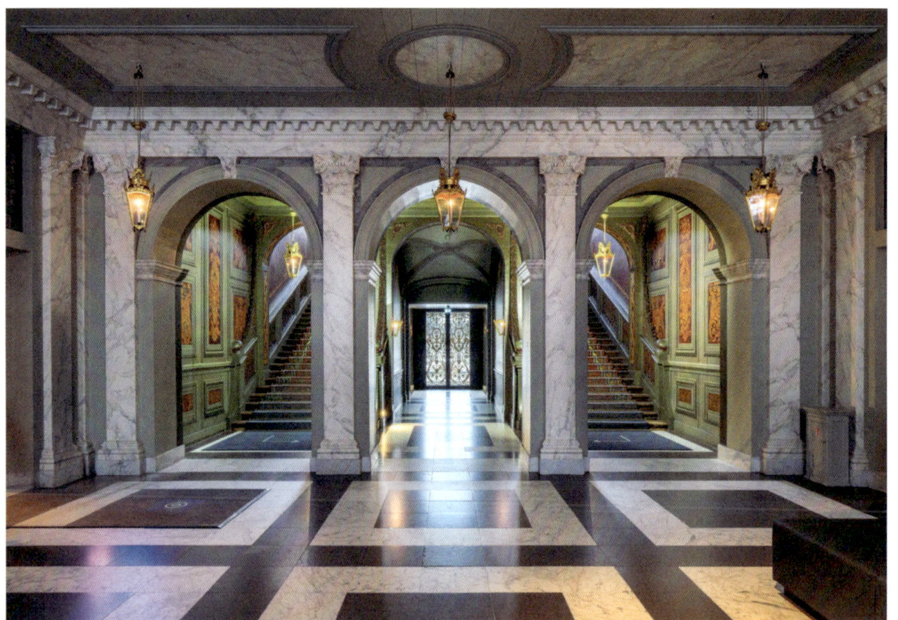

Willem and Mary's apartments were to the left and right of the Great Hall. To get there, every visitor had to go through the vestibule and then up the Grand Staircase to the first floor. What Willem showed on the walls tells us a lot about how he wished to present himself to visitors in his double role as king and stadtholder. The paintings played an important role in the ceremonial welcoming of guests. Murals were used in this way not only at palaces, but also at 17th-century country houses around Europe. They animated spaces that connected different parts of the building, such as passageways and staircases, and caught the attention of those passing by. Paintings could convey a message about both the personal tastes and the political ambitions of the residents, transforming a space from a simple thoroughfare to a place full of meaning.

Lost and found

The mural existed in its original form for over a century. The first round of restorations probably took place between 1728 and 1737. We do not know whether the image was altered at that time.

↑ The Grand Staircase seen from the vestibule.

→ One of the figures on the west wall of the Grand Staircase.

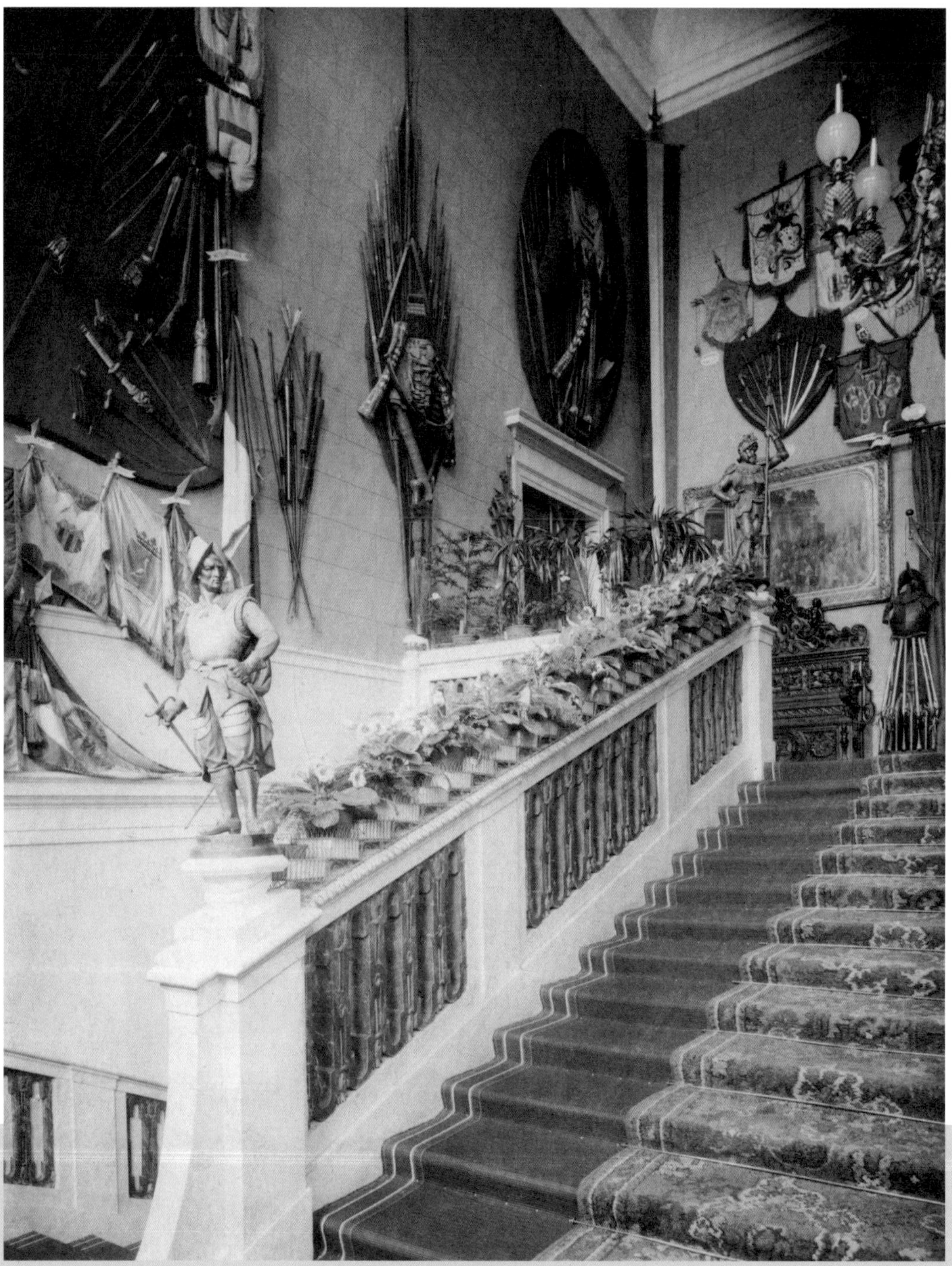

↑ The Grand Staircase in 1895, with a layer of white plaster.
→ Queen Wilhelmina, dressed in white mourning attire, posing on the Grand Staircase after the death of her husband Prince Hendrik in 1934.
→ Willem Fabri photographed before 1898, showing two designs for Paleis Soestdijk.

The first metamorphosis took place in 1806-1810, when the Netherlands was governed by King Louis Napoleon (1778-1846), brother of the French emperor. In accordance with French neoclassical taste he had both the outside walls of the palace and the walls of the Grand Staircase rendered with white plaster. The plaster remained intact for almost the entire 19th century. Coats of arms, weapons and paintings were hung on the walls. This remained so until the early 1890s, when the plaster began to flake off.

When she ascended the throne in 1898, Queen Wilhelmina decided to return Paleis Het Loo to its original 17th-century style. This radical restoration project revealed parts of the old staircase mural. It was however in such poor condition that it could not be restored, so it was decided that the mural should be reconstructed. Decorative painter Willem Adrianus Fabri (1853-1925) from Rotterdam was commissioned to carry out the work. He produced interior paintings for other palaces during the same period. Between 1900 and 1902 Fabri and his assistants recreated the entire mural in oil on large canvases, based on fragments that had survived and the print made by Marot, the original designer.

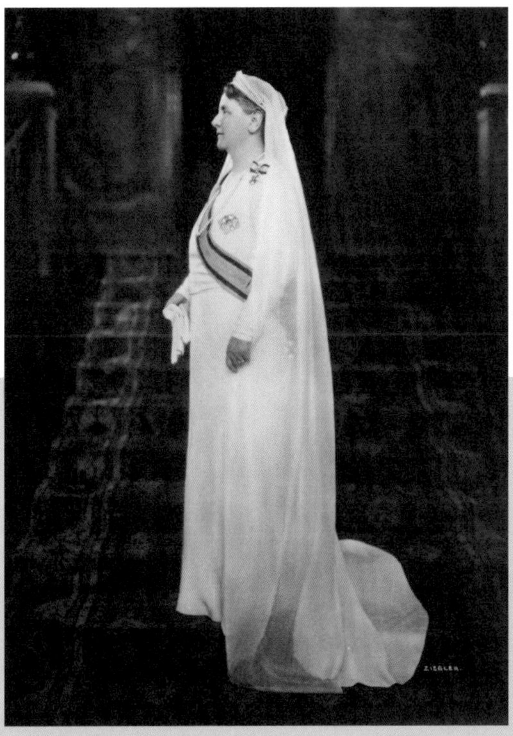

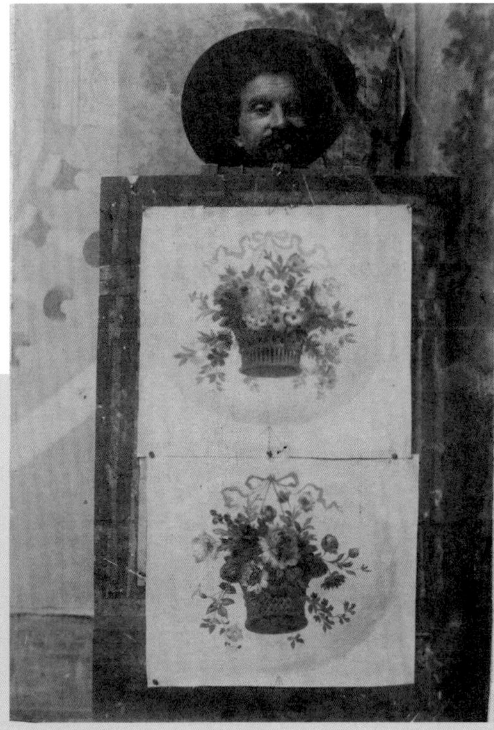

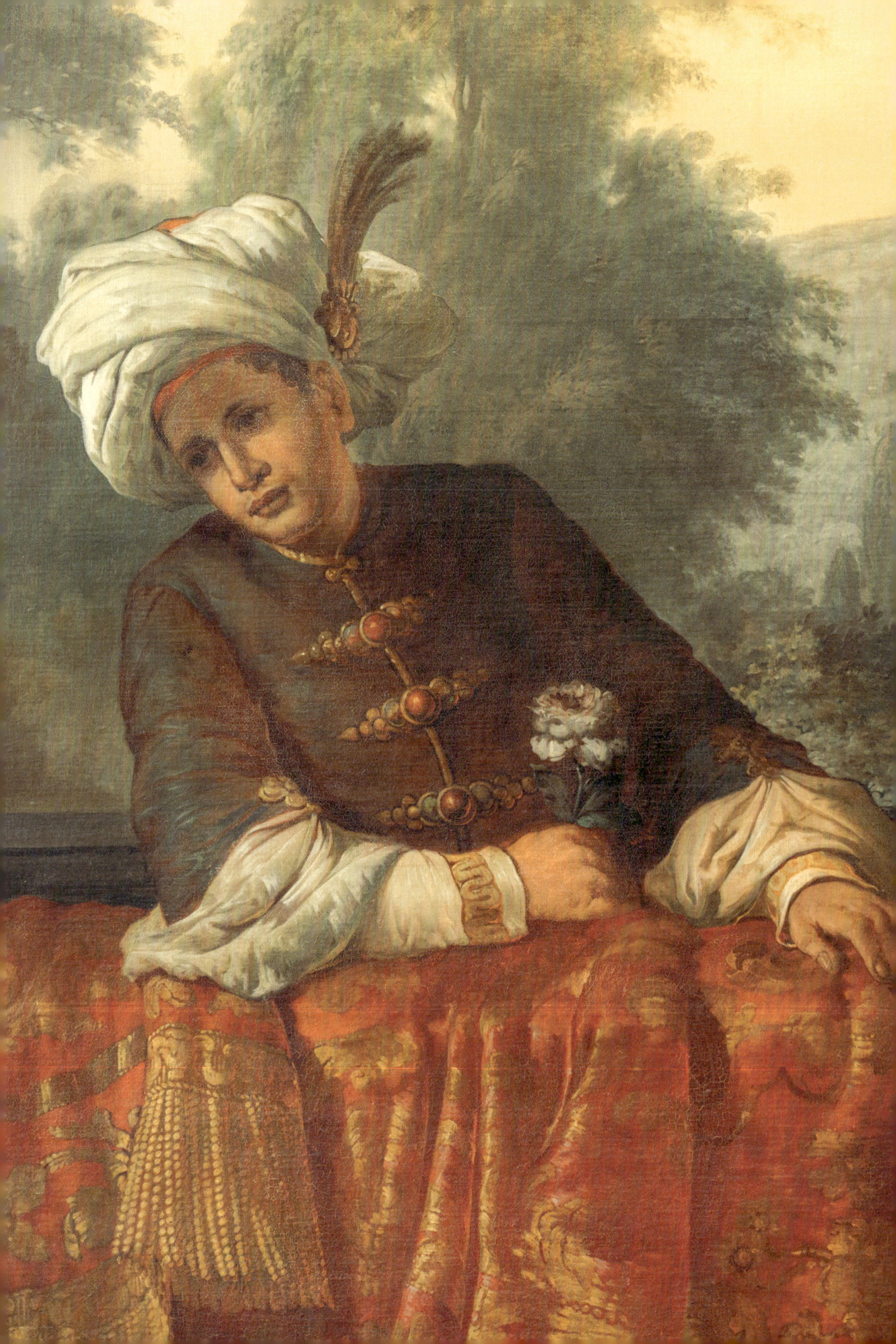

Welcoming the World

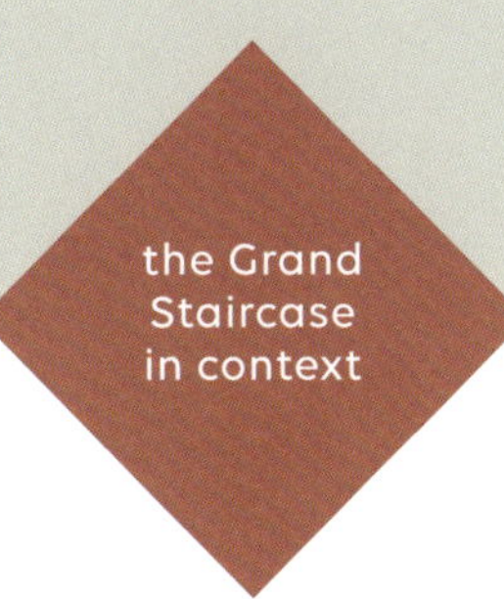

The palace's lavishly decorated Grand Staircase was very important to Willem and Mary. It showed that they were part of a cultural elite, with contacts all over the world. Willem's decision to entrust the design to Daniël Marot would later have consequences abroad, particularly in England.

Huis Honselaarsdijk

The Dutch Republic already had a tradition of interior painting prior to Marot's arrival in the Netherlands. These paintings would sometimes include Asian elements. At the time, Asia was seen as another world entirely, very far away. Interior decorations that referred to Asia reflected the client's status and connections. There are clear similarities between Marot's design for the Grand Staircase at Paleis Het Loo and earlier 17th-century interior painting schemes. One example is a design, never executed, for a mural by Cornelis Holsteyn (1618–1658) at Huis Honselaarsdijk, a palace belonging to the stadtholder in Zuid-Holland province. The drawing features a balustrade and figures wearing turbans.

The previous occupants of Huis Honselaarsdijk, Stadtholder Frederik Hendrik (1584-1647) and Amalia of Solms-Braunfels (1602-1675), were Willem III's grandparents. Willem and Mary later used the palace themselves. Several artists worked on the decoration of Honselaarsdijk in 1653. Some of them

← **One of the figures on the Grand Staircase.**

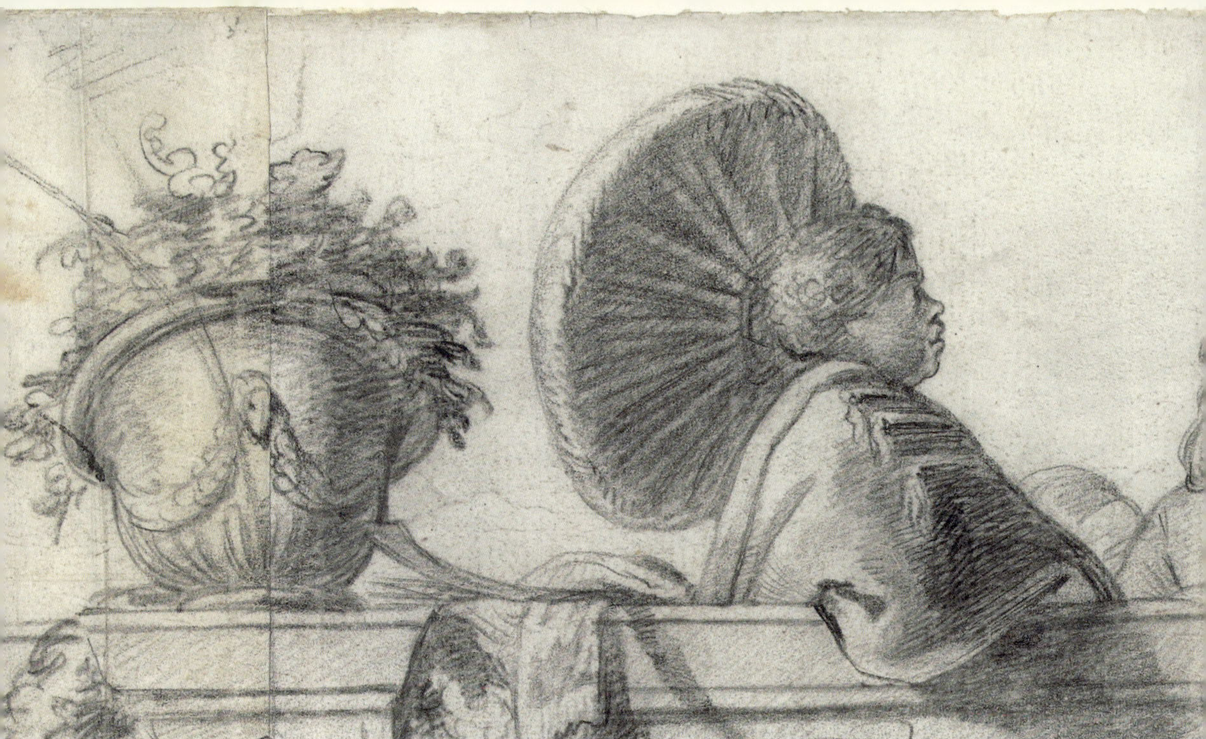

Cornelis Holsteyn produced this drawing of figures leaning on a balustrade decorated with garlands for Huis Honselaarsdijk between 1633 and 1638.

might have been familiar with Holsteyn's design and reused some elements of it. One of these painters was Andries de Haen (active 1639-1674).

The Binnenhof

Before he went to work on Huis Honselaarsdijk, De Haen worked on one of the largest surviving ceiling paintings in the Dutch Republic. The painting graces the Senate chamber at the Binnenhof, the Dutch parliament building. Architect Pieter Post (1608-1669) produced the design, which was commissioned by the States of Holland and West-Friesland.

De Haen and his son-in-law Nicolaas Wielingh (1640-1678) executed the ceiling painting. Some parts of it appear to be related in terms of its visual idiom to the later painting for the Grand Staircase at Paleis Het Loo. People of various ethnic backgrounds peer in through circular openings in the ceiling. They come from regions with which the Republic had economic or political ties. Their presence is a reference to Holland's global power and maritime dominance at the time. Wielingh painted the onlookers, while De Haen was responsible for the frames and the decorative details.

The figures – 'generic types' rather than actual historical individuals – symbolised 'all the peoples of the world'. Such images were popular among

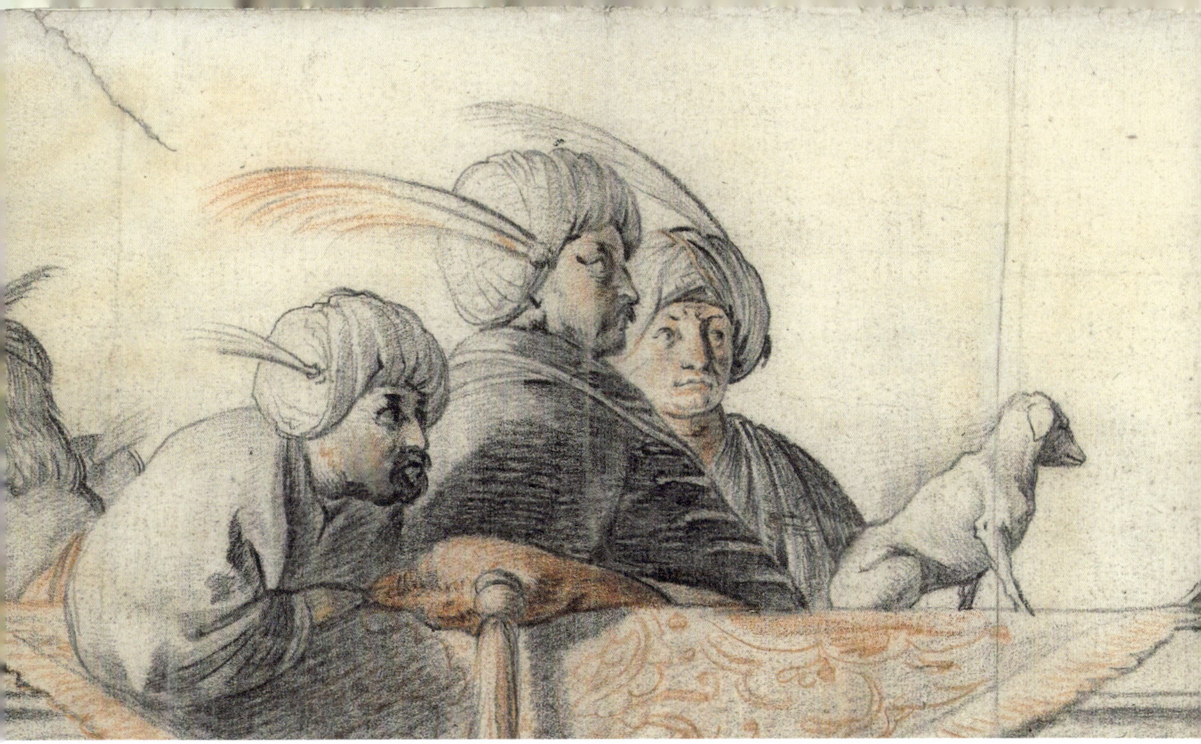

aristocrats throughout Europe, where political power and global trade were closely intertwined.

The peoples depicted include both important trading partners and rivals of the Dutch Republic. The figures are French, English, German, Spanish, Italian, Polish and Russian. Two groups are particularly striking. The first presents a clichéd depiction of Ottoman Turks wearing turbans. They are being led into the meeting of the States of Holland and West-Friesland by a figure who appears to be Italian, probably Venetian, with long hair and a feathered cap. The second group represents Persia. The Phrygian cap worn by the woman in the middle was associated with that country.

In the mid-17th century the Ottoman Empire was a powerful player. The fact that Ottomans are depicted on the ceiling of the Binnenhof illustrates the importance of trade with the east at that time, mainly through the eastern Mediterranean. A special trading organisation had been established for Mediterranean trade in Amsterdam 25 years before this painting was made. Yet the new Republic was not an equal in its relations with the Ottoman Empire, whose great size and military might made it highly influential. The presence of the Persian Empire beside the Ottomans on the ceiling is a striking feature. It may be that those who commissioned the painting wished to show that they were making clever use of the rivalry between these two empires in order to secure their trading interests at both imperial courts.

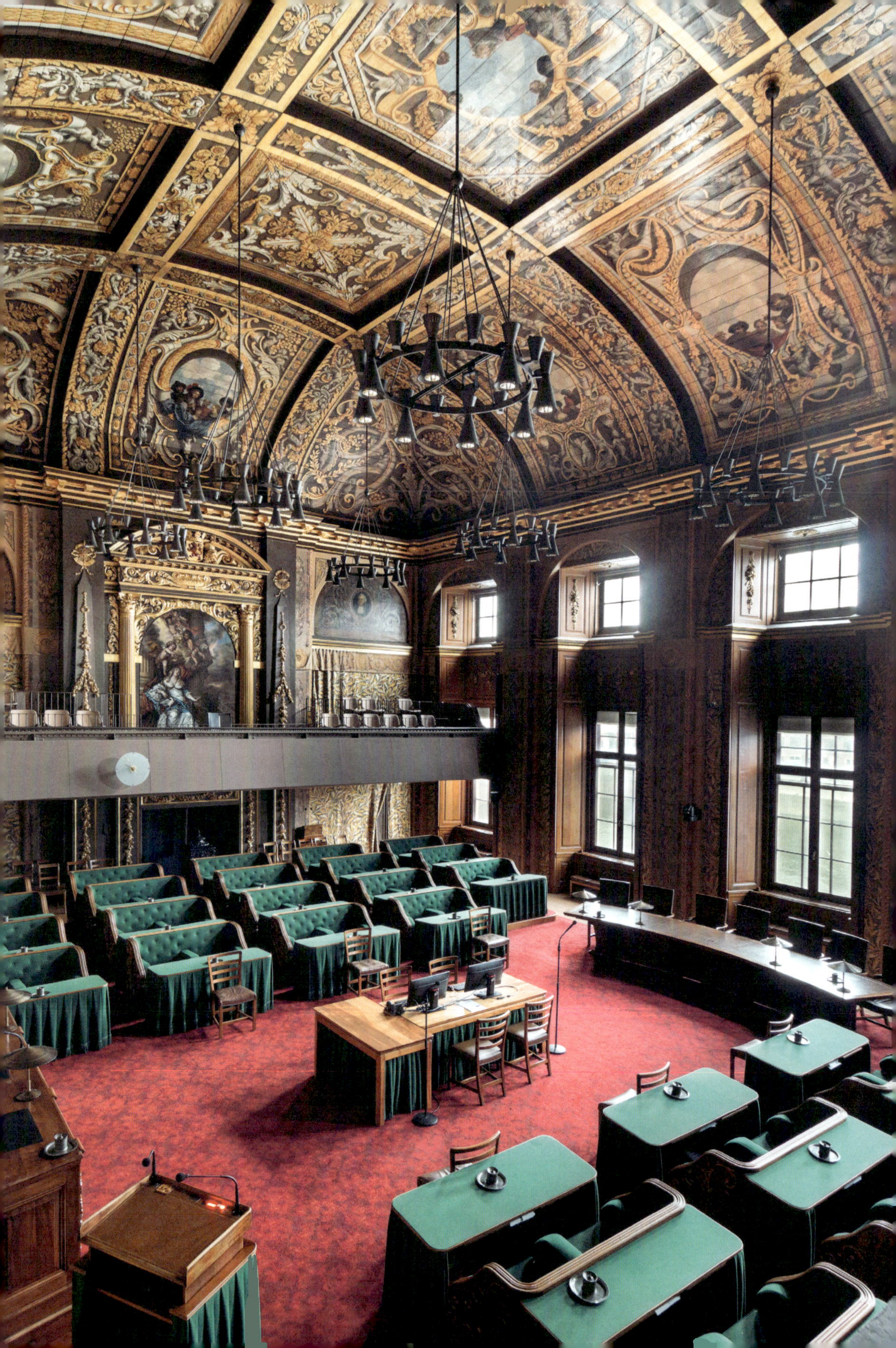

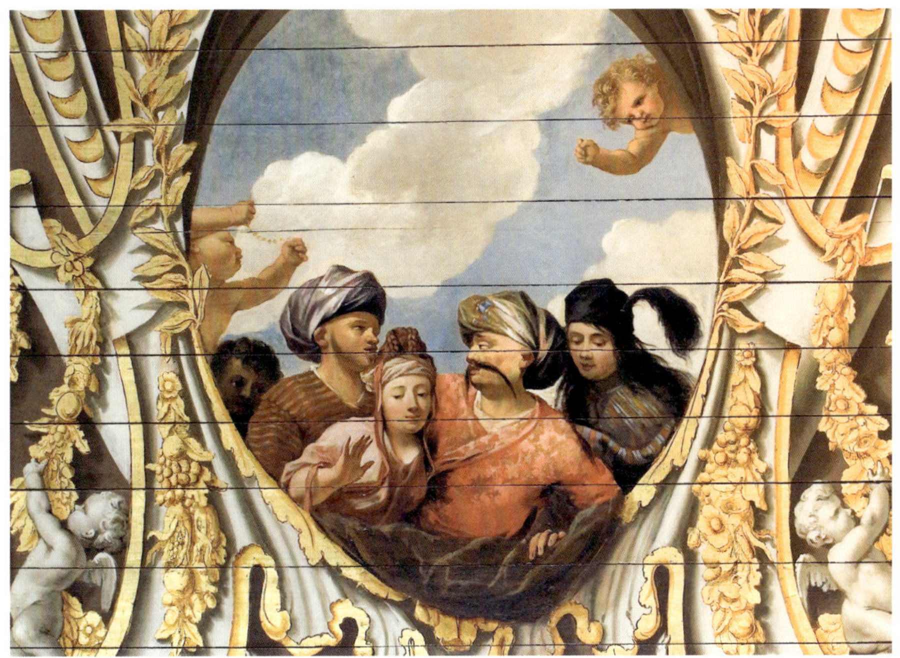

The Turkish group painted by Nicolaas Wielingh.

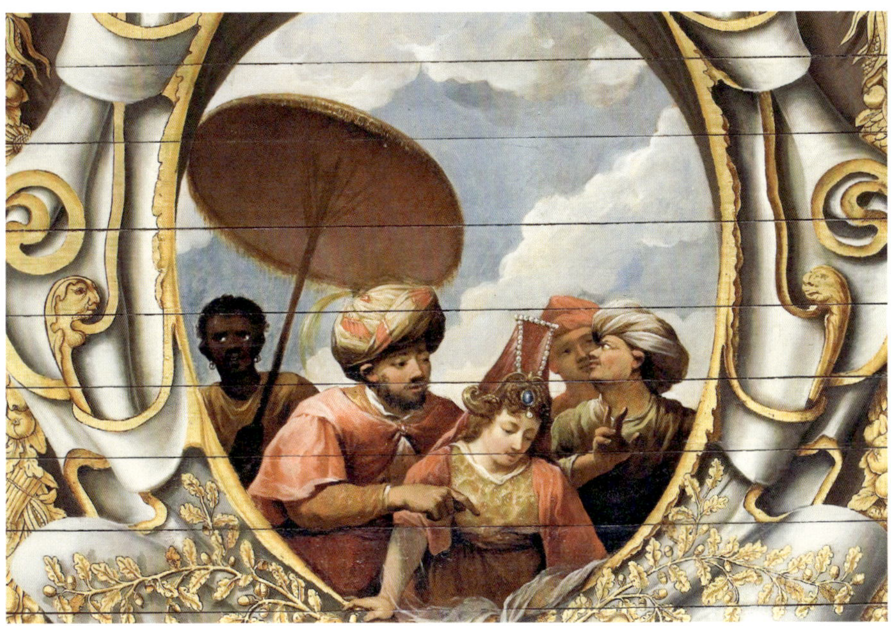

↑ The Persian group painted by Nicolaas Wielingh.

← The 17th-century Senate chamber with ceiling paintings by De Haen and Wielingh.

The ceiling in the chamber at the Binnenhof and the staircase mural at Paleis Het Loo are part of the same 17th-century painting tradition. There also appears to have been a connection between the artists. Nicolaas Wielingh, one of the painters who worked on the Binnenhof, was the master of Robbert Duval, who transferred Marot's design to the walls of Paleis Het Loo. As court painter to Willem III, Duval had many contacts in Hague art circles. He had probably seen the figures that Wielingh had painted on the ceiling at the Binnenhof before he started working on Paleis Het Loo.

Around 1680, some thirty years after the decorations at the Binnenhof were painted, the motif of 'people from all four corners of the earth' was incorporated into a monumental painting once more. Not in a public space this time, but at a private residence: Trompenburg House in 's-Graveland, built for Admiral Cornelis Tromp (1629-1691) between 1675 and 1678. There, an unknown artist decorated the cupola in the Great Hall – known as the 'Trompzaal' – with a crowd of figures from different parts of the globe, underlining Tromp's status as a celebrated admiral and man of the world. Willem III was among the honoured guests who visited Trompenburg.

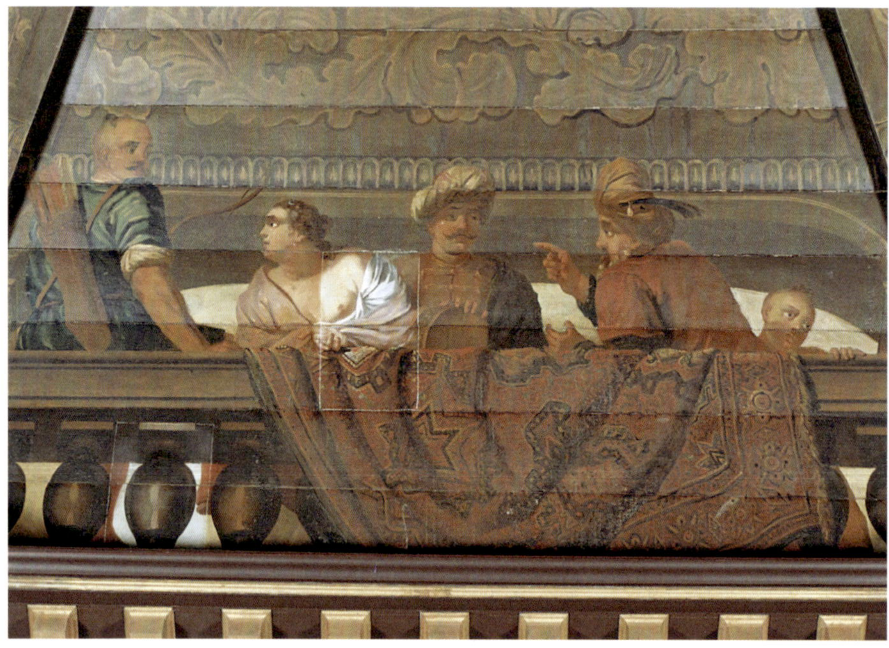

↑ Detail of the ceiling painting from c. 1680 in the 'Trompzaal', with Ottoman-looking figures conversing behind a balustrade.

→ The domed 'Trompzaal' at Trompenburg House.

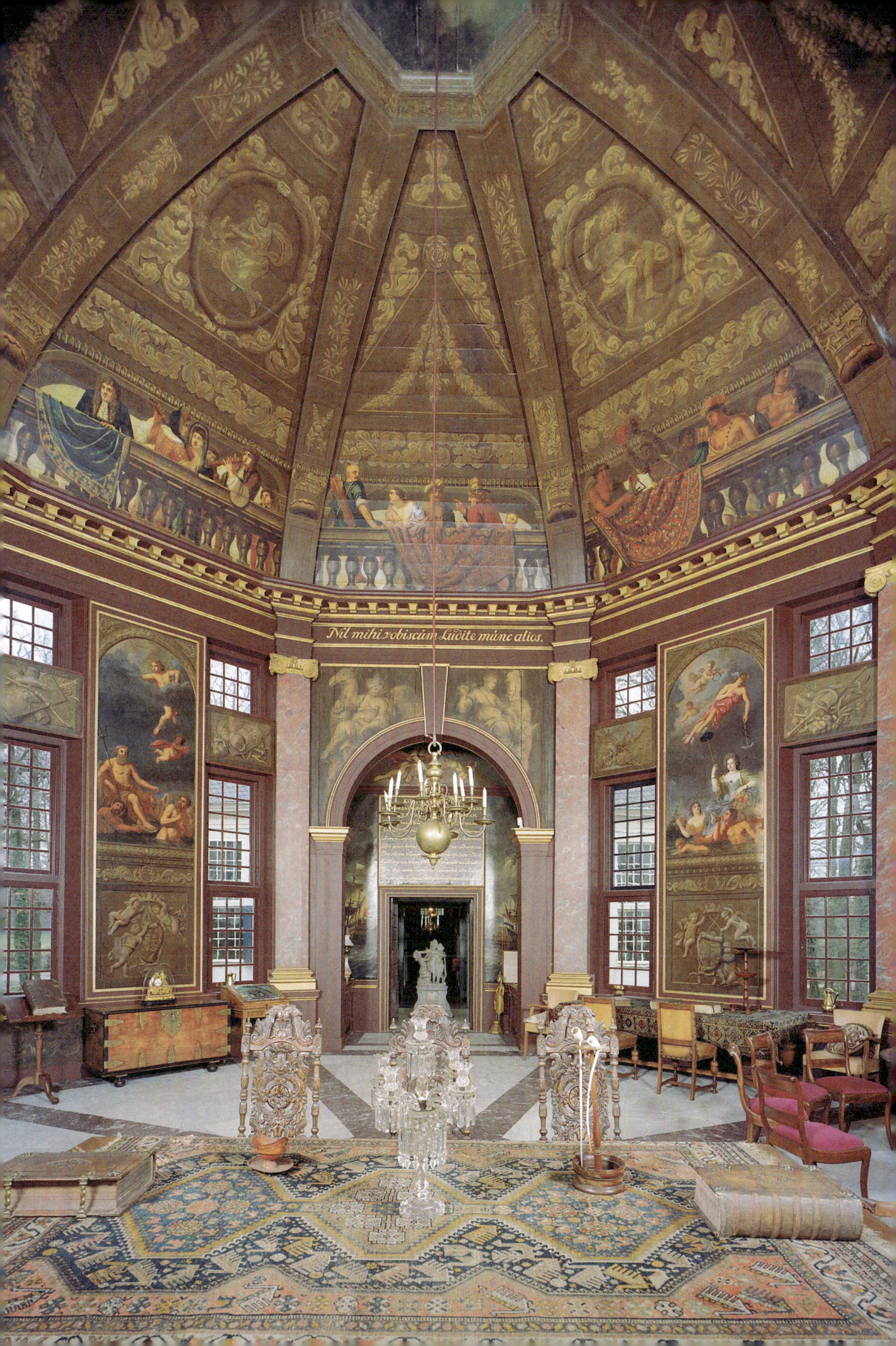
Nil mihi vobiscum Ludite nunc alios.

The Ambassadors' Staircase at Versailles

Similar developments were occurring in interior painting in France during this period. This is interesting, as both the designer and main executor of the painting at Paleis Het Loo were inspired by French tradition. Marot was born in Paris and grew up among artists who were involved in the decoration of the Palace of Versailles. Robbert Duval also had a French background. In other words, Dutch and French influences met at Paleis Het Loo.

Perhaps the most important example for the paintings on the walls of the staircase in Apeldoorn was the famous 'Escalier des Ambassadeurs', the Ambassadors' Staircase in Versailles. Architect Louis Le Vau (c. 1612-1670) designed the staircase for King Louis XIV (1638-1715) of France. It was built between 1672 and 1679 and decorated by leading painter Charles Le Brun (1619-1690). This was approximately fifteen years before the completion of the mural at Paleis Het Loo. The Escalier des Ambassadeurs was demolished in 1752, but we know what the staircase and the mural looked like thanks to etchings made by French printmaker Louis Surugue (c. 1686-1762).

The walls of the Escalier des Ambassadeurs were decorated with numerous figures that symbolised the peoples of the four parts of the world known at that time: Europe, Asia, Africa and America. This highlighted France's global influence. A large proportion of the decoration was devoted to Louis's victory in the Franco-Dutch War (1672-1678), in which he fought Stadtholder Willem III. As the name suggests, the staircase at Versailles was intended for use by foreign ambassadors who were en route to the Hall of Mirrors to meet the king. No high-ranking foreign guest would be able to overlook Louis's military successes and the grandeur of his palace.

The figures above the entrance, directly opposite the first landing, are the most striking element of the Escalier des Ambassadeurs. Before the staircase was dismantled, a book of etchings by Louis Surugue was published, featuring 'different nations' in Asia and Africa. Le Brun's positioning of these figures clearly influenced the staircase painting at Paleis Het Loo.

↓ **The Escalier des Ambassadeurs in Versailles in an etching made by Louis Surugue in 1725, (p. 36-37).**

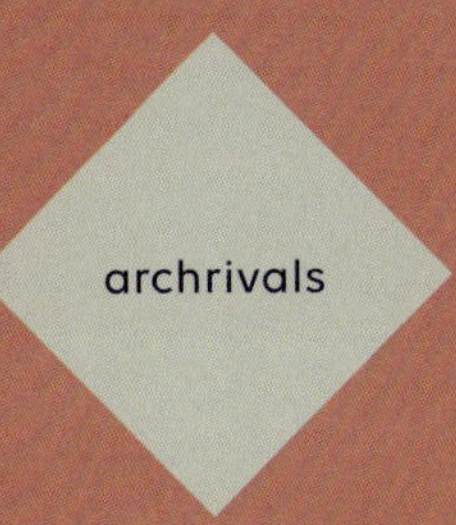

archrivals

The 'Sun King', Louis XIV of France, and Willem III were lifelong rivals. Willem was born in the year when his father, Stadtholder Willem II, died. This signified the start of the 'first stadtholderless period' (1650-1672) in the Dutch Republic. The regents, wealthy city administrators, were the new powers that be. But when the French invaded in 1672 – known in Dutch history as the 'Rampjaar', or Disaster Year – the Dutch sought a powerful leader to protect them. Willem III was appointed stadtholder like his father, grandfather and great grandfather before him. A stadtholder did not have absolute power like a monarch, but was the highest-ranking official in the Republic, in the service of its seven States. Willem III had mainly military duties, and was thus closely involved in foreign policy. He therefore took every opportunity to show that he could compete with or even surpass the French king. When he became King of England, Scotland and Ireland in 1689, he became his archrival's equal. The painted staircase at Paleis Het Loo confirmed his status.

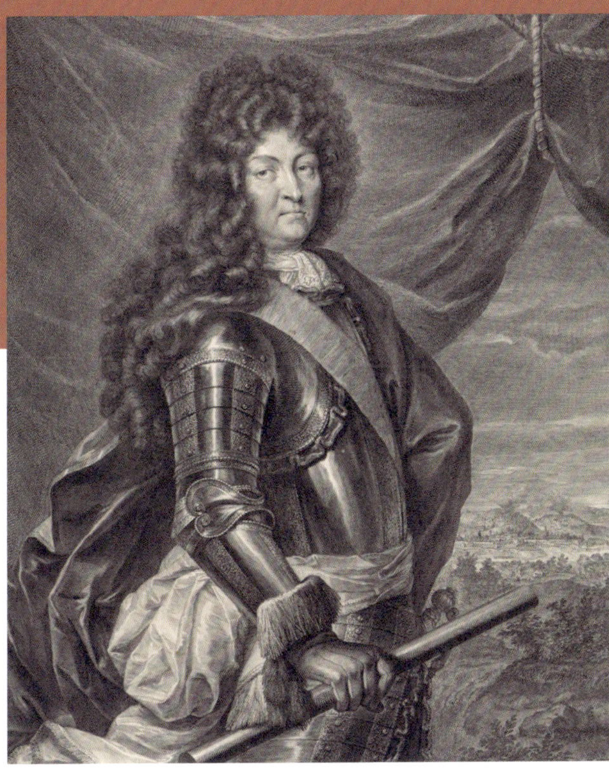

Portrait of King Louis XIV in armour, engraved by Gerard Edelinck after a painting by Jean de la Haye (detail).

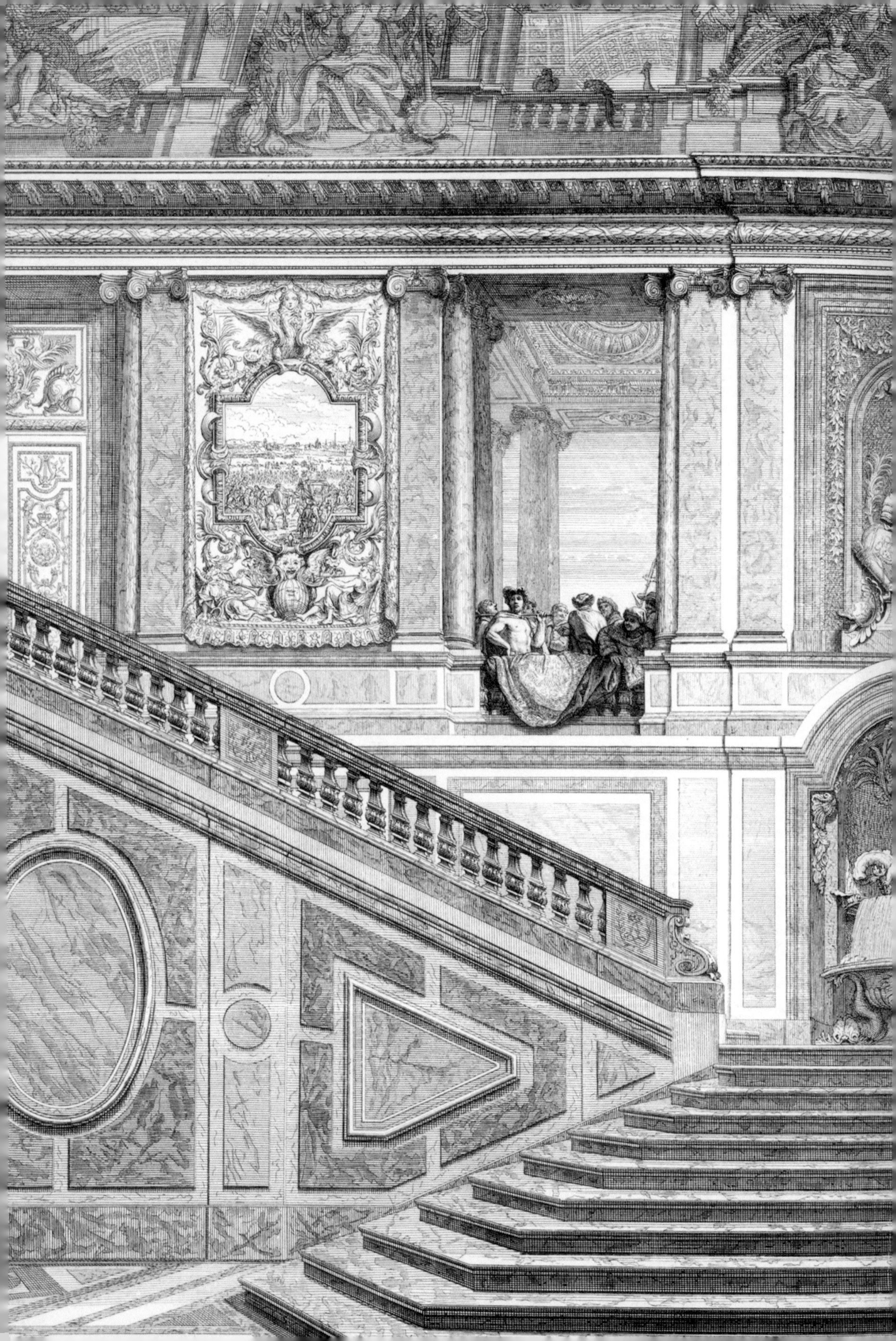

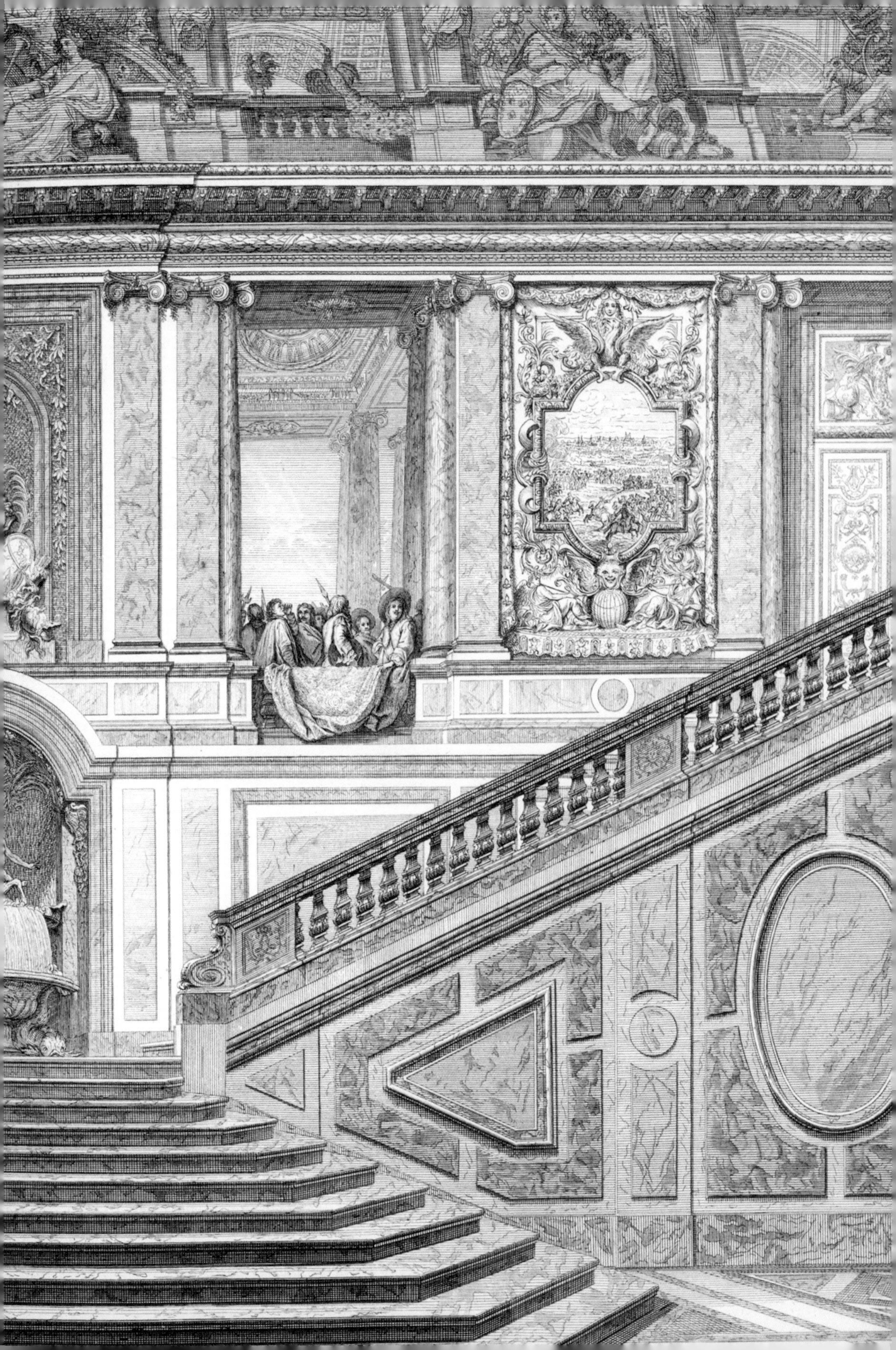

Marot saw it as a powerful symbol: foreign delegates seen observing incoming diplomats from behind lavishly decorated balustrades. This visual reference signified that Paleis Het Loo was a match for the powerful Versailles, and was thus entirely to Willem III's taste. Though the staircase at Paleis Het Loo was not only intended for the use of diplomats, it did have a similar function. It was designed to impress visitors and underline Willem's status.

The Queen's Staircase

Around 1680, the 'Escalier de la Reine', or Queen's Staircase, was built as a counterpart to the Escalier des Ambassadeurs. The new staircase led to the king and queen's apartments, and soon became the most frequently used staircase in Versailles. The Escalier de la Reine, which still exists, is clad almost completely in coloured marble. The wall beside the top landing was lavishly decorated with an image depicting an imaginary palace interior. The real marble balustrade appears to continue into the painted scene, enhancing the illusion that the space really does continue beyond the wall. Behind the painted balustrade is a man wearing a fantacised Ottoman robe. He is holding a tulip in one hand, while the other points to a vase containing an exuberant floral arrangement. Two painted landscapes used to complete the décor, but they were removed in the 19th century.

It is likely that the two murals at Versailles inspired Marot's design for Paleis Het Loo. Both Daniël and his father, Paris architect and engraver Jean Marot (1619-1679), were members of the artistic circles associated with Versailles. Daniël had also worked for Jean Bérain the Elder (1640-1711), Louis XIV's lead designer, who was closely involved in the interior design of Versailles. Marot may have come into contact with the painters of the Escalier de la Reine via Bérain.

↗ Details from the etchings 'The Different Nations of Asia' and 'The Different Nations of Africa' by Louis Surugue, based on designs by Charles Le Brun.

→ The painted figures on the east and west wall of the Grand Staircase at Paleis Het Loo.

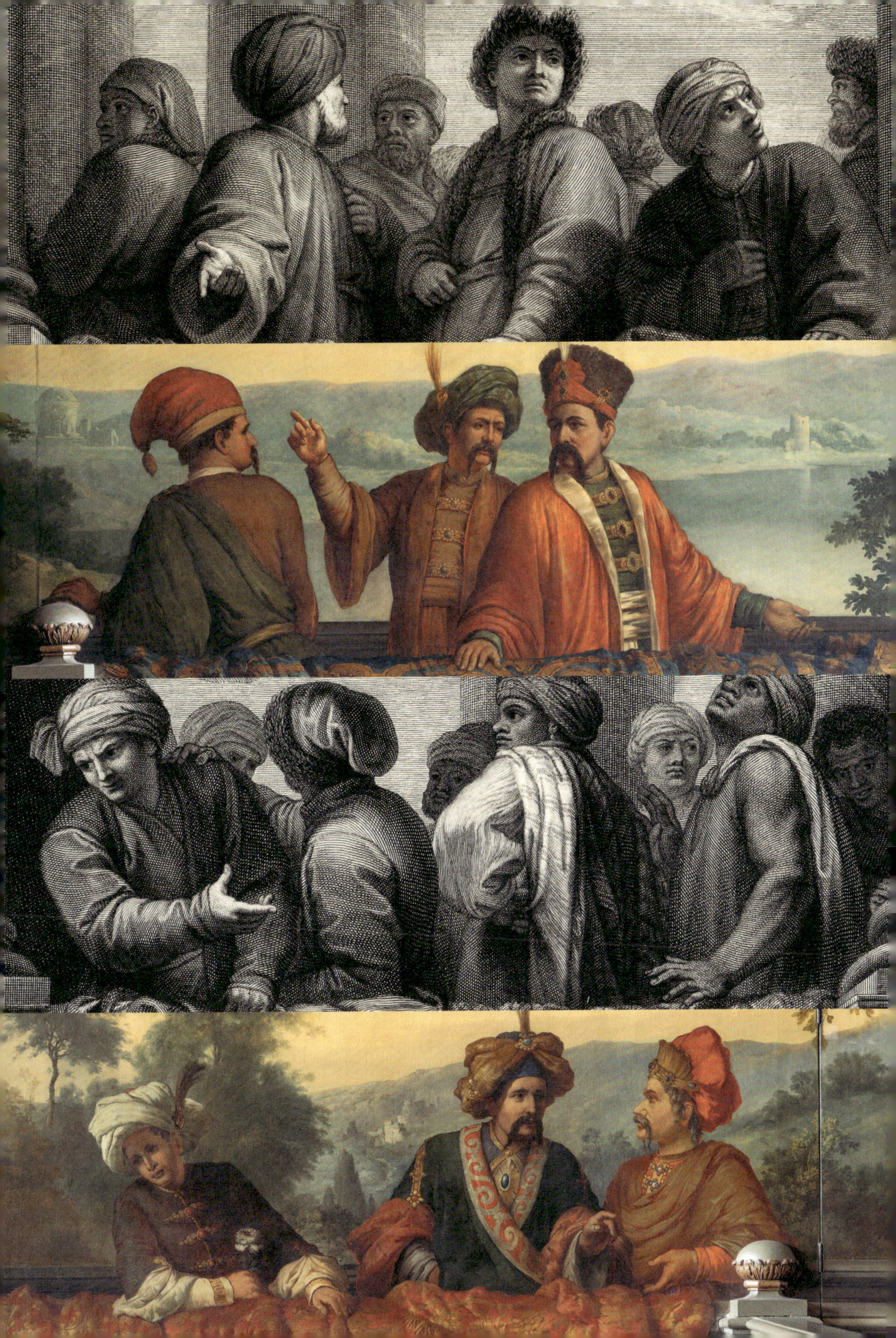

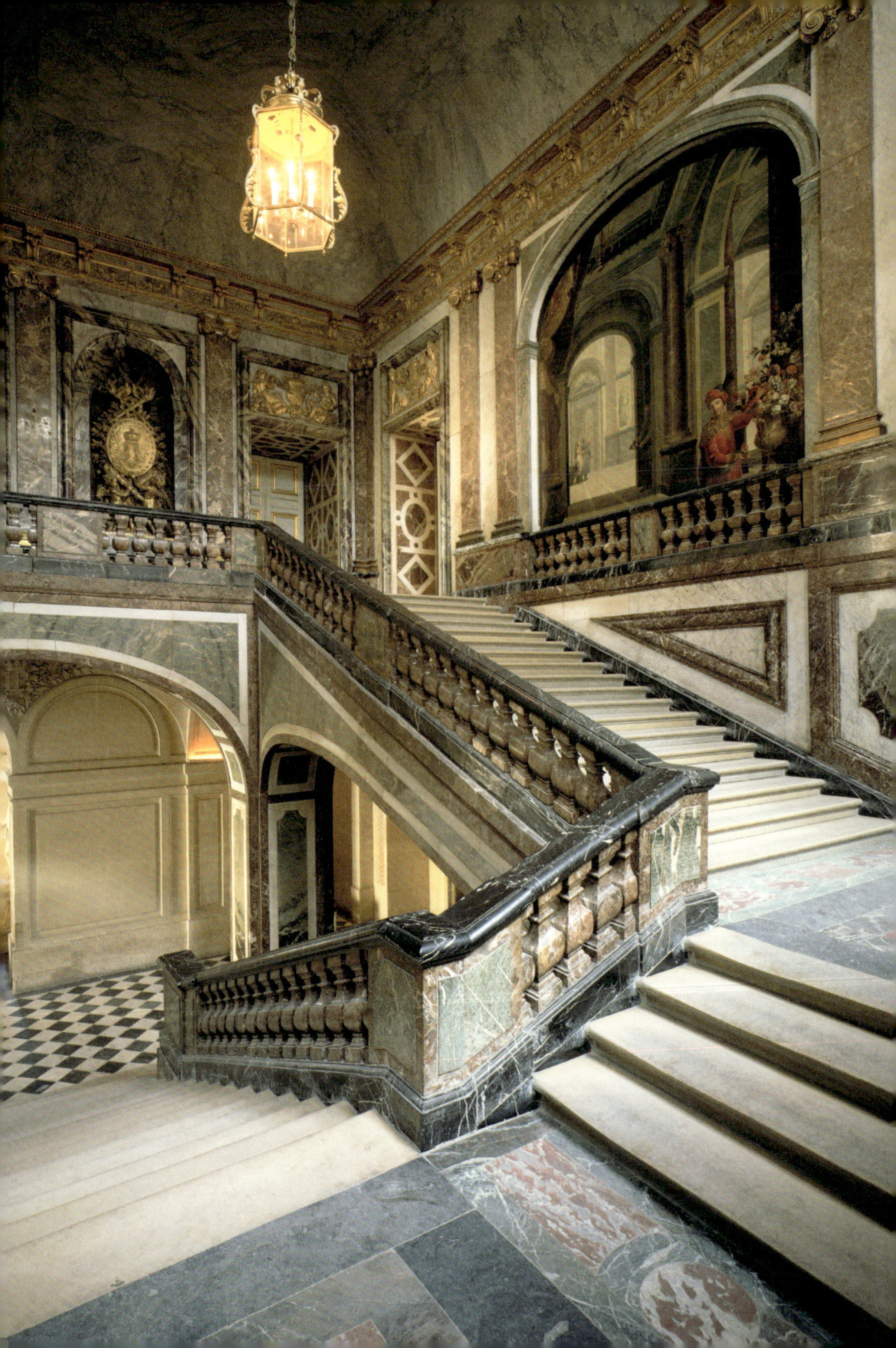

Hampton Court

Several years after the mural at Paleis Het Loo was completed, Robbert Duval went to work at Willem III's English court, housed at Hampton Court Palace. Daniël Marot had already been in England for some time, working mainly for Willem and Mary, though other aristocrats also gladly made use of his services.

The presence of Marot, Duval and other artists from the king-stadtholder's circle marked the start of a new chapter in English interior painting, boosted by Willem's patronage. In December 1700 the king even had a wooden scale model of the staircase at Paleis Het Loo brought to Hampton Court. Marot may have used it for inspiration when he designed the King's Staircase, the royal staircase at the English palace. The designs for Paleis Het Loo and Hampton Court cannot be seen in isolation from each other.

The King's Staircase by Antonio Verrio

Willem issued his first commission for murals at Hampton Court around 1700. A year later, work on the decoration of the King's Staircase commenced. Italian artist Antonio Verrio (1636-1707) painted a dynamic mythological scene on the walls.

Verrio's mural at Hampton Court depicts a story from classical antiquity, with references to Willem III as a great and powerful ruler. He is represented by the figure of Alexander the Great, king of a legendary empire. This impressive mural beside the staircase that led to his new London apartments allowed Willem to make a powerful visual statement. The work was probably made with a nod to, or perhaps even as a satire of, the famous Escalier des Ambassadeurs in Versailles. It was thus a subtle criticism of the pride and self-aggrandisement of his rival Louis XIV.

The visual scheme for the staircase was probably devised in consultation between the artist, Willem himself and Matthew Prior (1664-1721), a diplomat and poet who worked as the secretary at the British embassies in The Hague and Paris in the 1690s. He kept Willem informed of the artistic projects at the court of the French king, and had seen the famous Ambassadors' Staircase with his own eyes. His knowledge and experience probably played a key role in the design of the paintings for Hampton Court.

← The Escalier de la Reine at Versailles.

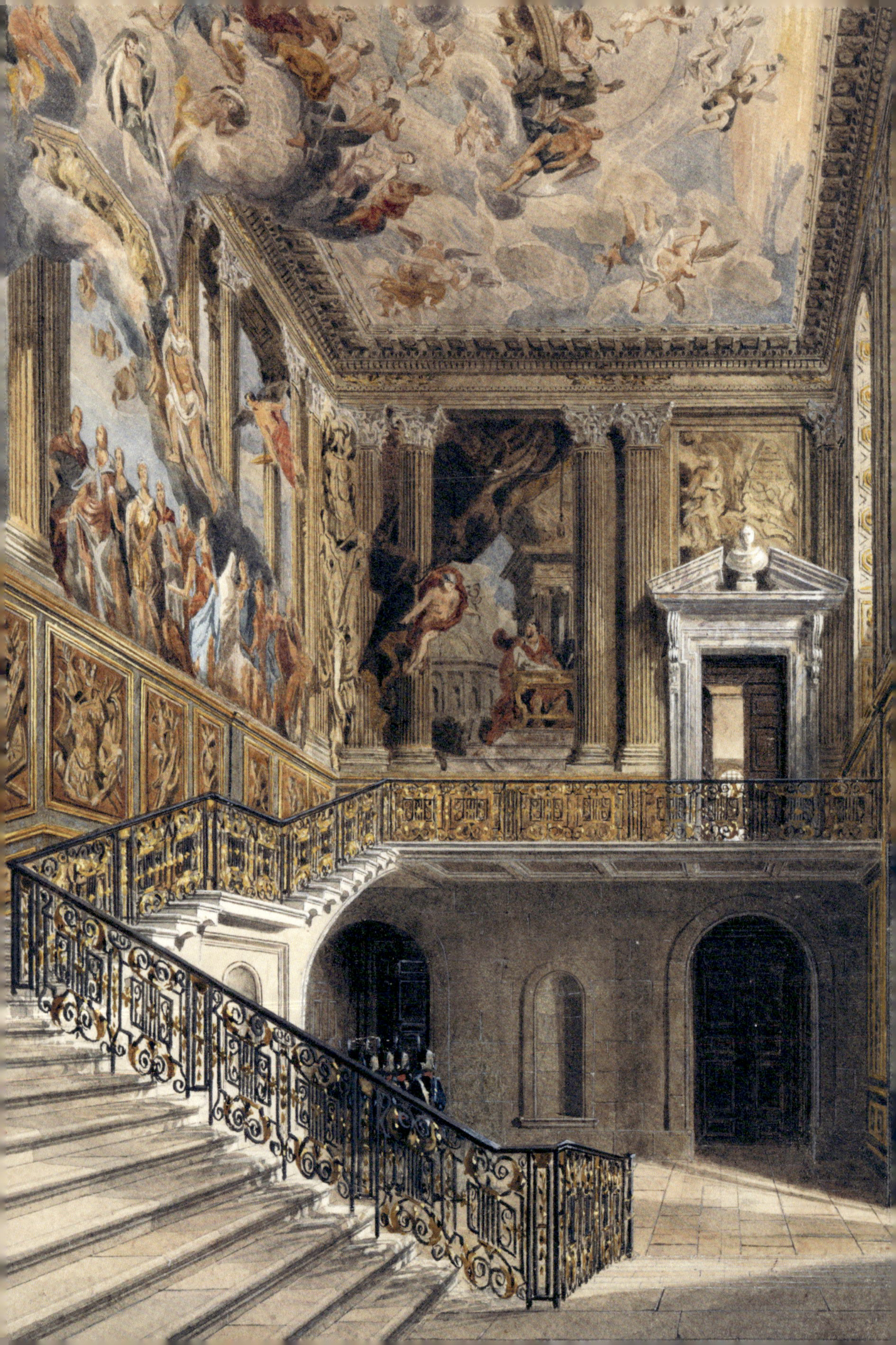

Franco-Dutch influences in England

Another artist who worked for Willem III at Hampton Court was Louis Laguerre (1663-1721). He was born in Versailles, where his father was in charge of the royal zoo. Laguerre had studied under Charles Le Brun at the art academy in Paris. He was probably familiar with the Escalier des Ambassadeurs at Versailles, which would inspire his later work.

Laguerre moved to England in circa 1683 and spent most of his career there. At first he worked alongside Antonio Verrio, but he soon received independent commissions for country houses in England. His Protestant clients had no objections to his Catholic background. Laguerre was pragmatic, too. He may have been godson to Louis XIV, but his work often featured English military victories over the French king. Willem III also commissioned him to work at Kensington Palace and Hampton Court. Willem was impressed by Laguerre and even offered him an apartment at Hampton Court. The crowning glory of his career came at the end of his life, when he completed two prestigious paintings at the famous stately homes Petworth House and Blenheim Palace.

Between 1718 and 1720 Laguerre made a mural for the staircase at Petworth House, commissioned by Charles Seymour, 6th Duke of Somerset (1662-1748). The painting depicts an symbolical victory procession by Seymour's wife, Lady Elizabeth Percy (1667-1722). She was a close friend of Mary II's. With its painted architecture, view to the sky and vase in the style of Marot beneath, the piece recalls the staircase painting at Paleis Het Loo. It also demonstrates how a group of artists associated with Willem III developed a visual idiom that was popular among the aristocracy. Willem visited Petworth in 1693, shortly after the completion of his own mural in Apeldoorn, and again around 1694-1695. As a result of his preference for a Franco-Dutch style and his support of artists like Marot and Laguerre, this style became widespread in England. Marot was a regular guest at Petworth. He worked on alterations to the house, which was given a new interior in Franco-Dutch baroque style between 1692 and 1748. The artists again looked to the court of Versailles for inspiration.

← Richard Cattermole painted this watercolour of the King's Staircase at Hampton Court in 1817.

Laguerre's masterpiece was the impressive mural and ceiling painting that he completed in circa 1720 for the Grand Salon at Blenheim Palace in Woodstock, southern England. Again, this project drew inspiration from Le Brun's famous Escalier des Ambassadeurs. This iconic example suited the grand ambitions of his client, General John Churchill, 1st Duke of Marlborough (1650-1722). Here, too, however, the influence of Marot's design for Paleis Het Loo becomes apparent in the open courtyard with its columns, vistas and figures from different parts of the world. The group of visitors from the Middle East is particularly reminiscent of the figures in the mural in Apeldoorn. At Blenheim, the foreign onlookers together represent 'the four corners of the world', and thus reflect the duke's global prestige.

↓ Posthumous portrait of Louis Laguerre, engraved by Alexander Bannerman (detail).

↘ The staircase at Petworth House.

→ The Grand Salon at Blenheim Palace with the painting by Louis Laguerre.

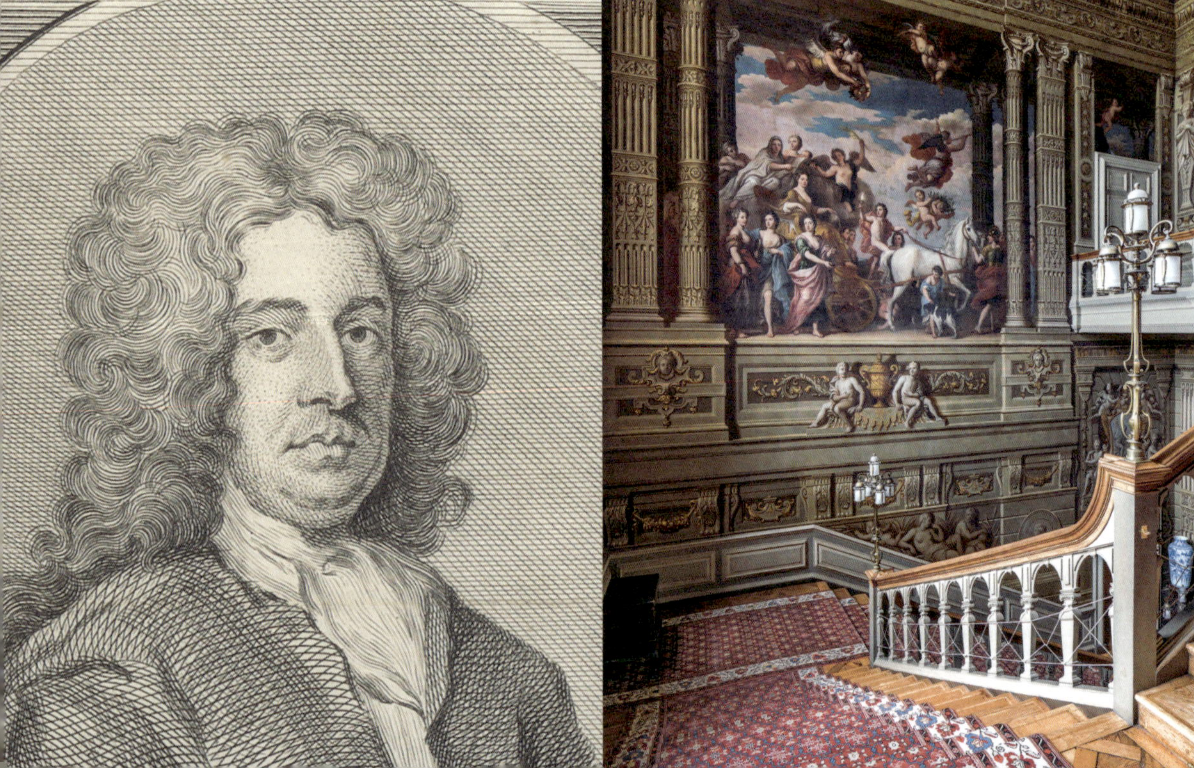

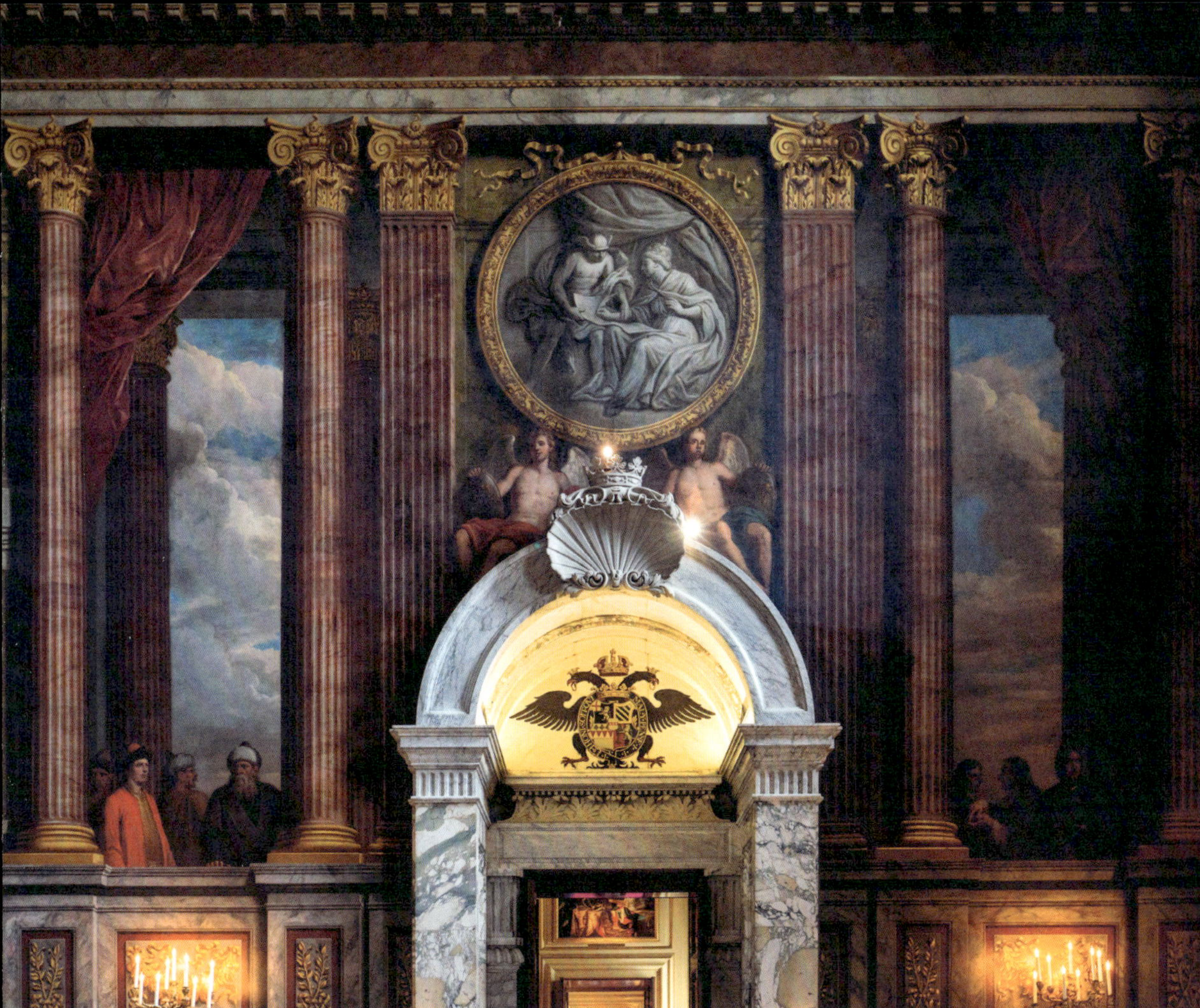

Murals painted before or after the painting at Paleis Het Loo generally include a wide range of figures from around the world. What makes the Grand Staircase in Apeldoorn unusual is the fact that the focus is on just seven figures from one empire. These are not recognisable historical figures, but characters. They all represent Ottomans. This choice was intentional. All of the murals discussed here were in places of power and prestige, whose decoration was chosen with care. To understand the significance of the seven male figures at Paleis Het Loo, we therefore need to consider international relations at the time when the mural was made.

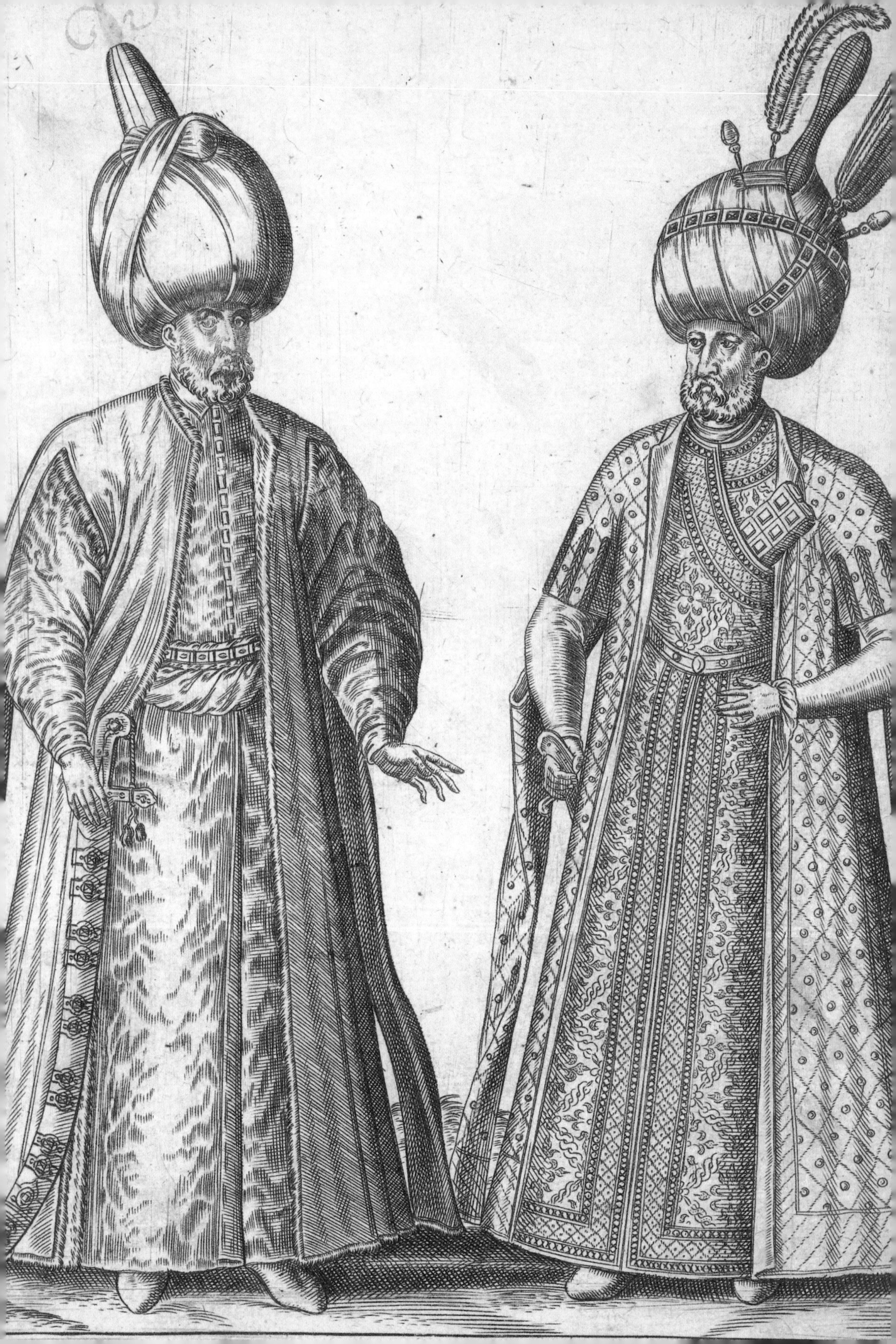

Landing between East and West

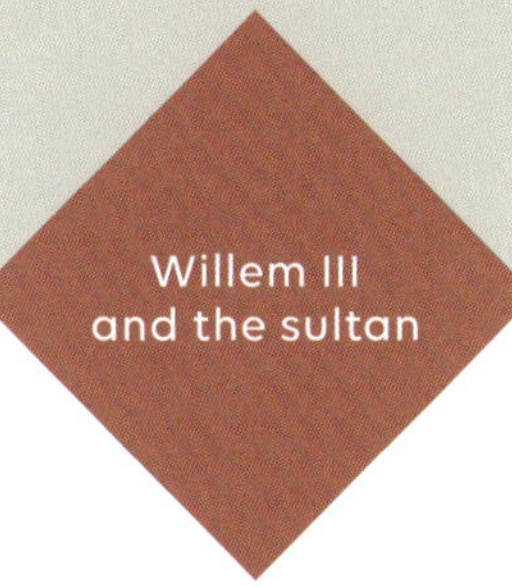

Europe's history has always been closely linked to that of the region we now know as the Middle East, the part of western Asia along the Mediterranean and North Africa. As early as the 14th and 15th centuries, Venice played a major role in this exchange, thanks to its lively trade with the East via Istanbul. The city, a hub where several important trade routes met, was Europe's gateway to Asia. Travel journals, diaries and translated historical texts gave Europeans their first impressions of 'Turks', 'Moors' and 'Africans'. Almost all the characterisations in these sources referred to inhabitants of the vast Ottoman Empire, without any regard for its multicultural nature. Conquest of regions closer to Europe in the 16th and 17th centuries had enabled the Ottoman Turks to expand their territory well beyond their capital Istanbul. They even reached Vienna, which they unsuccessfully attempted to take on two occasions, as they sought to extend their power into Central Europe. Vienna was in a strategic location on the border of the Habsburg Empire, to which a large proportion of Europe belonged, and was the gateway to the rest of Europe. At its height, the mighty Ottoman Empire extended from the Red Sea to the Black Sea, from Mecca to Budapest, and from Baghdad to Algiers. The Dutch Republic started engaging in independent trade with the Ottomans in the early 17th century. The fact that the Ottomans were prepared to trade with the new state gave it status and legitimacy in its struggle for independence from Spain.

← Two high-ranking Ottoman officials depicted in a 1581 costume book by Abraham de Bruyn (detail).

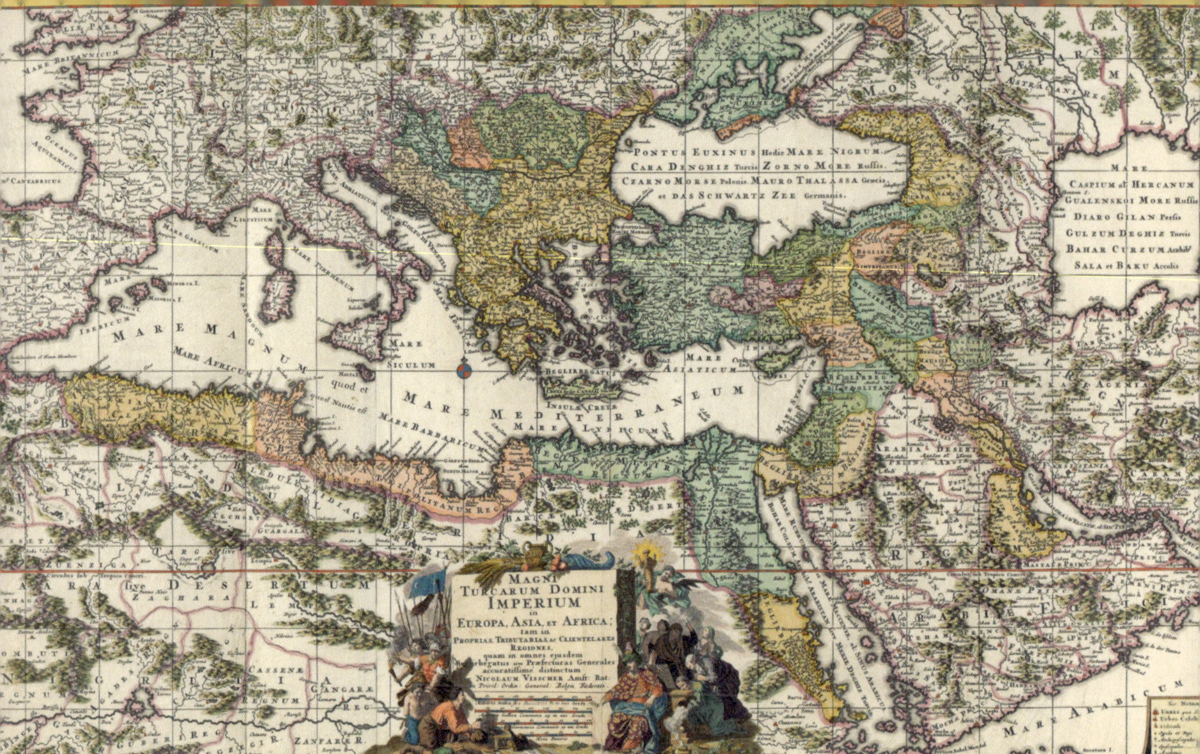

Map of the Ottoman Empire in the second half of the 17th century.

The Empire of the crescent moon

A large number of books about Turkish customs and the history of the Ottoman Empire were published in the 16th and 17th centuries, both in the Dutch Republic and elsewhere. The picture presented in these publications was often ambiguous and sometimes negative. Fear and contempt echoed in the words of European authors, with the occasional trace of admiration. The Islamic empire, often referred to as the empire of 'the Turk' or 'the Mohammedan', was depicted as a problem: a powerful opponent that posed an existential threat to Christian Europe.

Artists also helped shape Europeans' image of the Ottomans. Depictions of 'Turkish dress', intended to represent Ottoman attire, were a novelty to western audiences, and quickly became popular. The images mainly appeared in costume books. These collections of prints were sometimes based on the observations of travellers and pilgrims, but often they were compiled using existing images, whose provenance was not always clear. They were not, therefore, entirely reliable. In many cases artists blindly perpetuated existing stereotypes, or let their imaginations run loose with them.

Slowly but surely, European monarchs started to realise how important the Ottoman Empire had become to European politics and trade. Rather than constantly engaging in conflict, they increasingly sought some manner of peaceful coexistence. The Ottoman Empire even occasionally emerged as an unexpected ally to Calvinist and other Protestant groups in parts of the Habsburg Empire like Austria and Hungary. This strategic collaboration later became known as 'Turco-Calvinism'. The Turks sought in this way to use their influence to undermine the power of the Catholic Habsburgs, the influential European dynasty that for centuries had governed Austria, Spain and the Holy Roman Empire, which encompassed a significant proportion of Central Europe.

There was similar anti-Catholic feeling in the Low Countries during the Dutch Revolt (c. 1566/1568-1648), when a number of regions in the Netherlands rose up against Spanish rule. A popular slogan at the time was 'rather Turkish than Papish', indicating a preference to live under Ottoman rule rather than Catholic rule. Men wore crescent pendants or earrings engraved with the slogan as a sign of their allegiance, referring to the crescent moon as the symbol of the Ottoman Empire. The fashion was rekindled in the second half of the 17th century, probably under the influence of the Republic's new enemy: Catholic France with its absolute monarch, Louis XIV.

Diplomatic ties between the Republic and the Ottoman Empire dated back to 1612, when the sultan first gave Dutch merchants access to the Ottoman market. Relations between the two states were largely cordial. Trade with the eastern Mediterranean, also known as the Levant, was an important element of Dutch maritime commerce. Around the height of trade with the Levantine, in 1688, no fewer than 25 Dutch companies were operating in the Turkish port of Smyrna (today's İzmir) alone.

The growing European interest in the East was also reflected in visual culture, including at court. Daniël Marot designed Turkish tents and pavilions as garden ornamentation, for example – the first of their kind in western Europe. King-Stadtholder Willem III was also influenced by the trend, and hung a map of the Ottoman Empire in a passage between his bedchamber and private apartment.

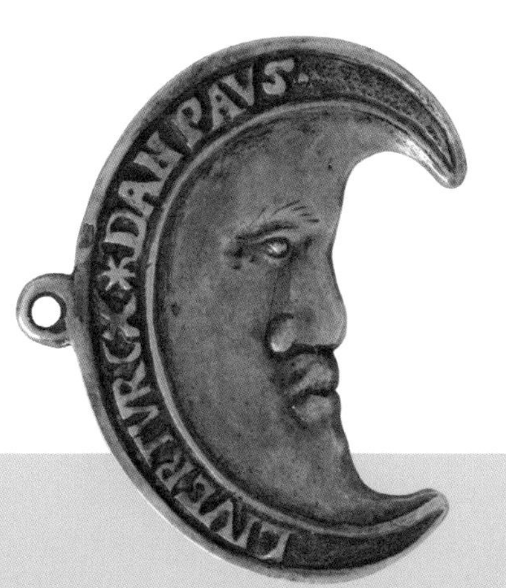

Silver pendant from 1574 with the inscription LIVER TVRCX * DAN PAVS, 'rather Turkish than Papish'.

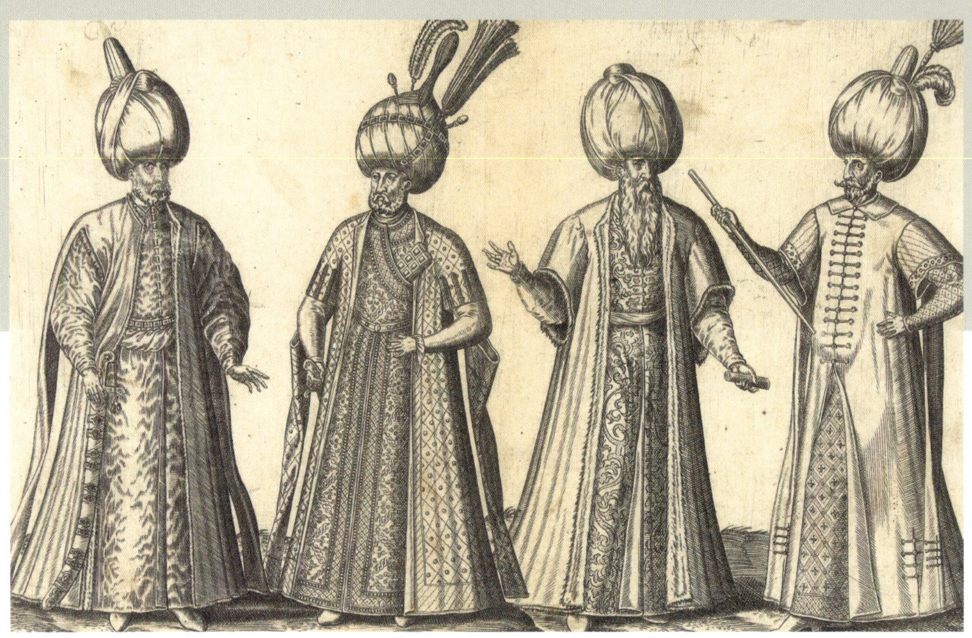

Ottoman dignitaries in a 1581 costume print by Abraham de Bruyn. He copied several of the figures, including that of the Sultan himself, from other artists.

Ottoman attire

In the second half of the 17th century, even more books were published about the Ottoman Empire. Many originated in France, which was developing ever closer ties with the Ottomans during this period. This probably meant that Daniël Marot and Robbert Duval, both of whom had French origins, drew much of their inspiration for their designs for Paleis Het Loo from French sources. The books were popular, and written in their mother tongue. Yet Dutch publications will have influenced them, too. Books about the Ottoman Empire were also published in the Republic, particularly following the Turks' second Seige of Vienna in 1683, and Marot and Duval may have used them.

This is not to suggest that the picture presented in their mural is a realistic one. The clothing worn by the men at the balustrades appears to differ markedly from that actually worn in the Ottoman Empire. Above all, the painting shows how Europeans imagined that the inhabitants of that distant empire looked. The carpets hanging over the balustrades also bear little resemblance to typical Turkish or Persian rugs of the period, even though inventories of Willem III's possessions tell us that he owned several. The clothes were probably inspired by costume books, Marot and Duval turning to them in the absence of authentic examples, which were scarce and difficult for them to access.

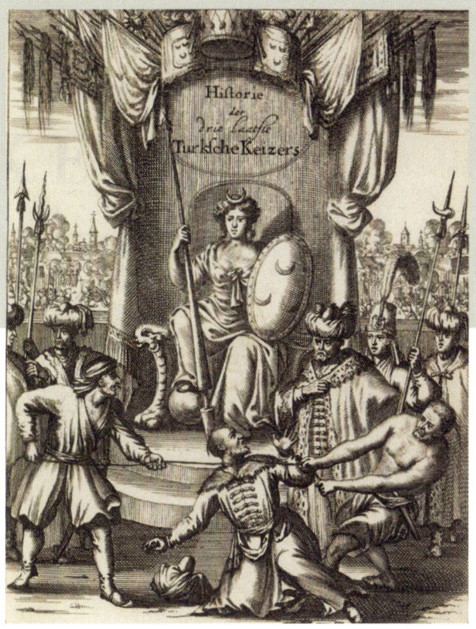

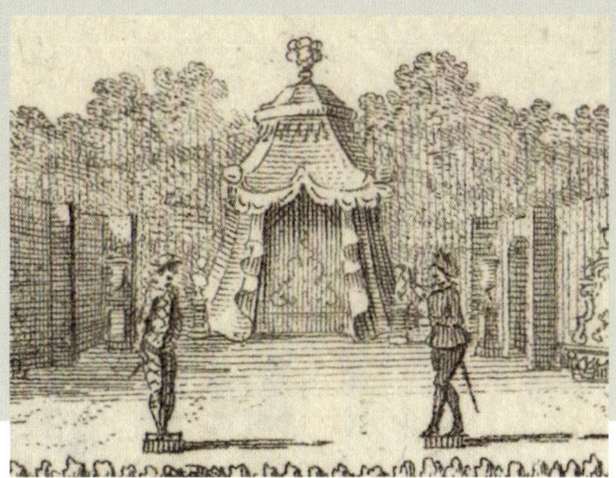

↑ A print by Hendrik de Leth showing a Turkish tent, likely designed by Marot, in the garden at Huis ter Meer in Maarssen (detail).

↖ Title plate from Paul Rycaut's 'Historie der drie laatste Turksche keizers' (The History of the Last Three Turkish Emperors) published in 1684, which was popular in the late 17th century.

A portrait of Thomas Hees (1634-1693) painted by Michiel van Musscher provides an example of more realistic Ottoman attire and rugs. Hees was the representative of the States-General to the governments of the Barbary States of Algiers, Tunis and Tripoli on the coast of North Africa. He wears a typical 'şalvar' (wide trousers that taper towards the ankles) and an 'entari', a long robe worn by both men and women. He also wears a waistband, or 'uçkur'. A 'vase rug' from Kirman, in present-day Iran, is draped over the table, and an Ottoman rug from Smyrna lies on the floor.

Research into the tradition of depicting Ottoman figures in the Dutch Republic in the 17th century has found that the seven men in the mural are not historical individuals. Yet they do include some authentic elements of traditional Ottoman dress. The two men in the centre on the west wall are wearing kaftans: dignified robe-like garments made of silk and other luxury fabrics, which were generally worn only by the elite, and on official occasions. They are wearing an entari secured with an uçkur beneath their kaftan, just like Thomas Hees in the portrait discussed above.

Furthermore, several figures appear to be wearing a 'yelek', a forerunner of the modern jacket, identifiable by the distinctive horizontal bands ('çapraz')

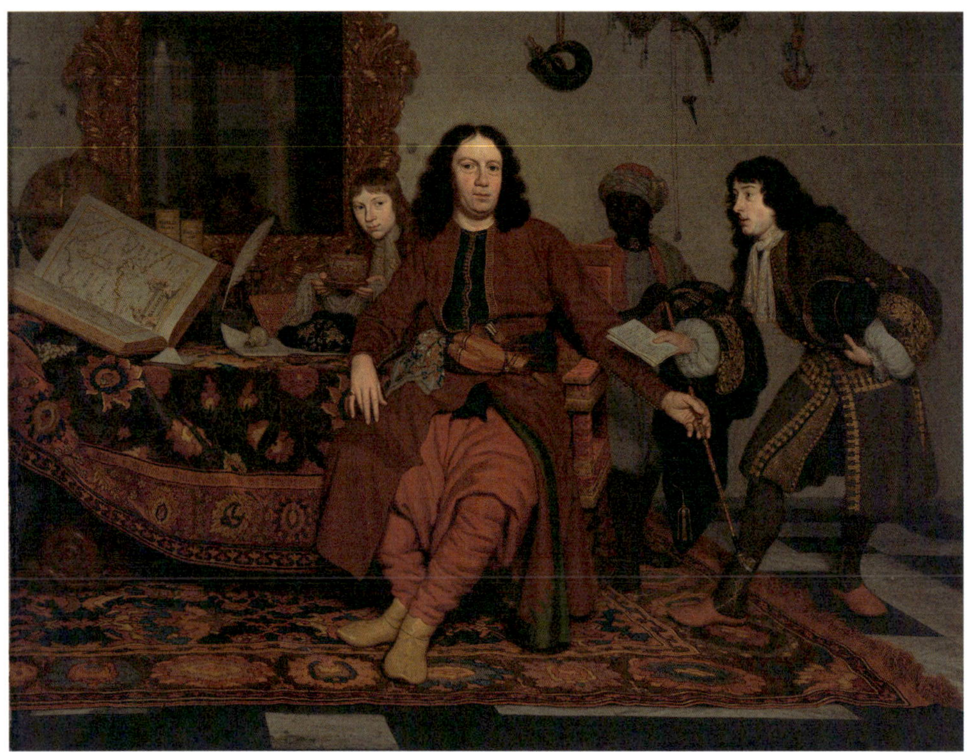

Portrait of Thomas Hees (in the centre), his servant Thomas and nephews Jan and Andries Hees, painted by Michiel van Musscher in 1687 (detail).

fastening it across the chest. The figure on the far right of the west wall may be wearing a 'kuşak': a broad sash worn around the waist, often over other garments. Finally, five of the men have feathered aigrettes in their turban or cap ('balıkçıl'). They were worn only at court, by the sultan himself and other high-ranking officials. One's outfit, and particularly one's headgear, was more than simply a fashion choice in the Ottoman Empire. Certain dress codes were exclusive to specific groups in society. What a man wore on his head showed at a glance what social class he belonged to.

There are few realistic depictions of Ottoman sultans from the 17th century. Images of people were long forbidden in Islamic art, for religious reasons. The portrait Jean Baptiste Vanmour painted of sultan Ahmed III is therefore highly exceptional. In the painting, the sultan wears a fur-trimmed kaftan fastened with çapraz, with an entari in the same colour underneath. On his head he wears a 'kâtibî', a turban skilfully wound round a simple headdress and decorated with a sumptuous feathered aigrette. The typical 'onion shape' of the turban indicates that it is an Ottoman style. The sultan's belt is beset

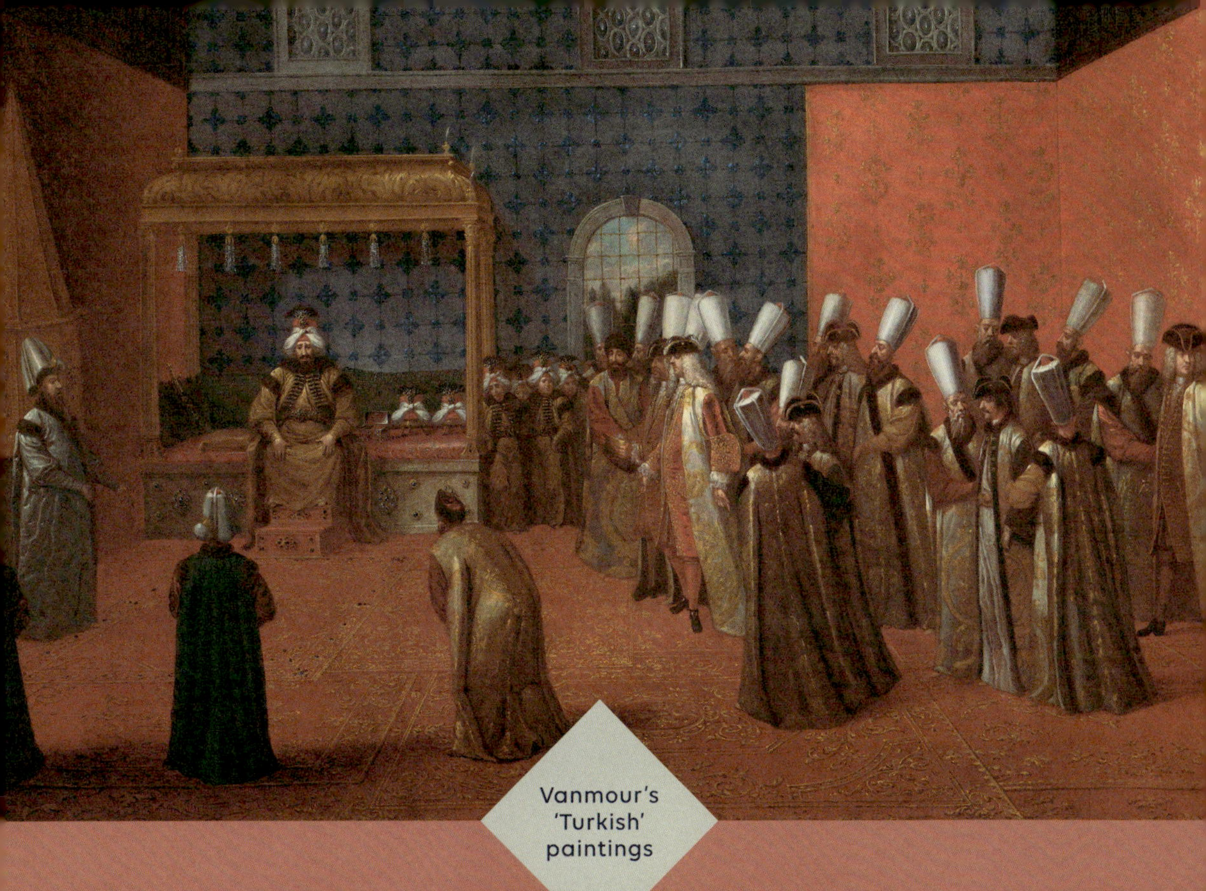

Vanmour's 'Turkish' paintings

Western artists often worked in Istanbul in the 16th and 17th centuries. However, they rarely had an opportunity to get a glimpse of the Ottoman court, let alone meet the sultan in the flesh. One artist was however lucky enough to do so: Jean Baptiste Vanmour (1671-1737), a Flemish-French painter who worked in Istanbul for many years. His paintings of people, interiors, towns and landscapes are an important cultural and historical source. In 1727 Vanmour accompanied the Dutch ambassador, Cornelis Calkoen (1696-1764), to an official audience with the sultan, Ahmed III. On this unique occasion, the painter was able to see the sultan with his own eyes. Afterwards, he painted a series of scenes at the Ottoman court for Calkoen. They included the reception of the ambassador and his retinue, and a full-length portrait of the sultan.

↑ **Vanmour's painting shows that the Dutch at the audience with the sultan are wearing kaftans, which they may have received as a token of hospitality, and also to conceal their western clothes.**

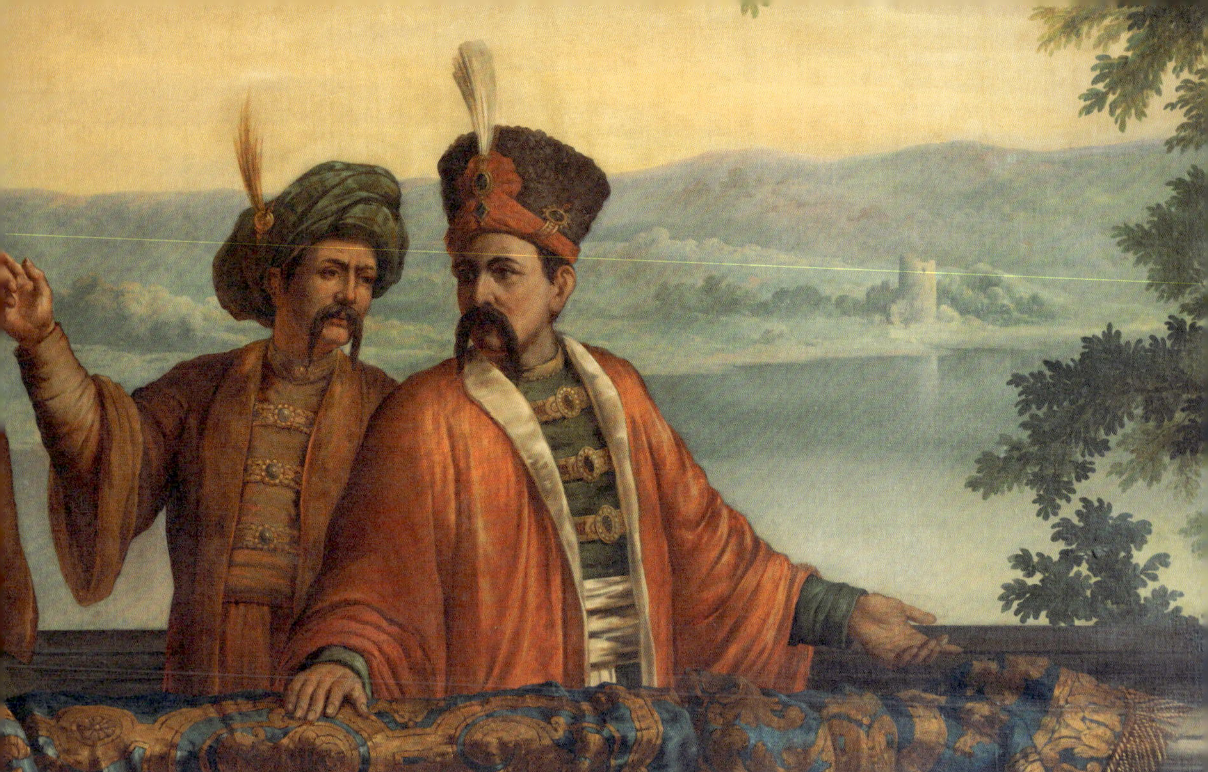

The men on the west wall are wearing kaftans and jackets fastened with a 'çapraz' – horizontal bands across the chest.

with jewels, emphasising his wealth and status. The similarities in the clothing – particularly the distinctive turban – between this portrait and the middle figure on the east wall at Paleis Het Loo are striking. It is highly likely that the man on the staircase represents someone of very high status.

Why did Willem and Mary have these seven striking men included in the staircase mural? What message did they want to convey? There are no known sources in which Willem III or Marot discuss, describe or explain the artwork, but other sources can help us understand the broader context in which the painting came about. International political relations in Europe in the late 17th century are a vital factor.

Political chess

Willem and Mary commissioned the mural at a time of great political unrest in Europe. A considerable portion of the continent was involved in some way or other in the Great Turkish War (1683-1699), when a European alliance, the 'Holy League', fought the Ottoman Empire. This was Europe's response to the Ottomans' failed attempt to take Vienna in 1683.

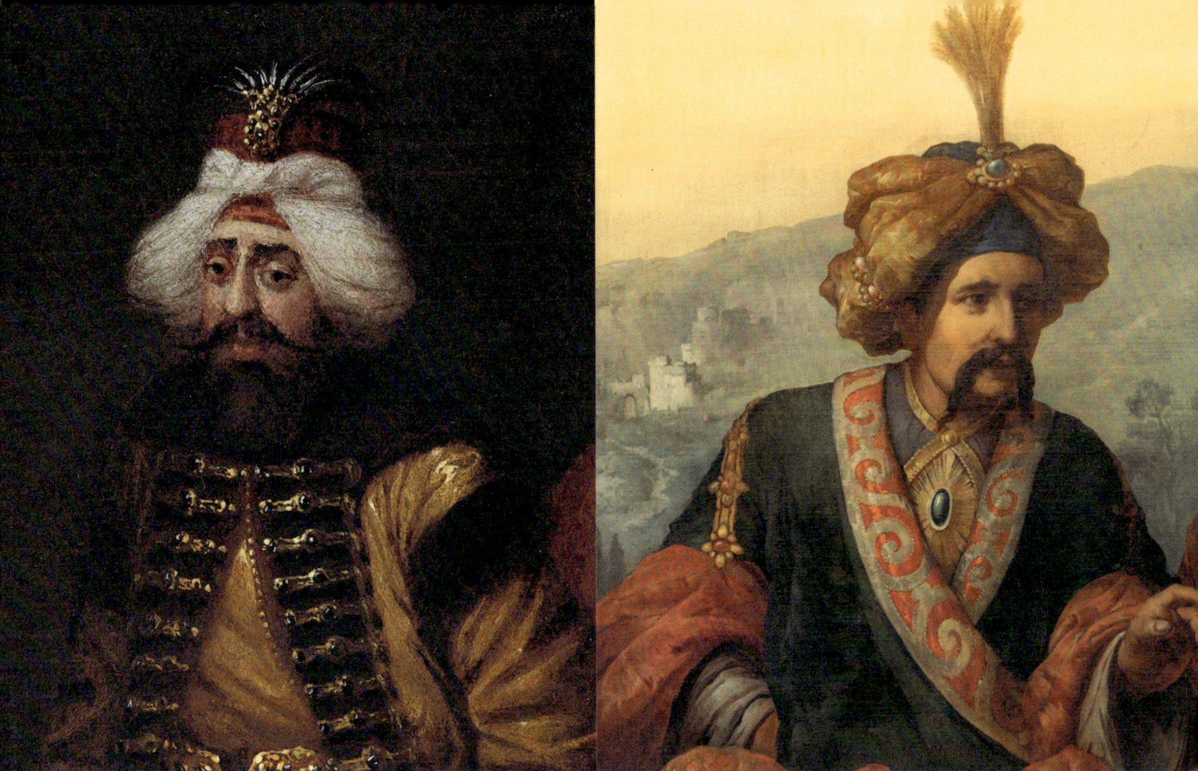

↑ Vanmour made this portrait of the sultan, Ahmed III, between 1727 and 1730 (detail).
↗ The man on the east wall of the Grand Staircase.

France was not part of the Holy League, as it had been working towards a renewed alliance with the Ottomans since 1673. The Holy Roman Empire, the loose association of European states in Central and Eastern Europe ruled by Emperor Leopold I (1640–1705), was however involved in the war. The emperor was a key ally of Willem III in his fight against the French king, Louis XIV. The Dutch Republic and England stayed out of the Turkish war, in order not to jeopardise trade with the Ottoman Empire.

At the same time as the Great Turkish War, Europe also faced the Nine Years' War, in which a coalition of European powers, including the Dutch Republic, England and the Holy Roman Empire fought France. Willem III played a key role here as the driving force behind the alliance and a central figure in the battle against Louis XIV, his lifelong rival. The Nine Years' War eventually turned into an economic disaster for the Republic, causing major disruption to its trade with the Levant, among other things.

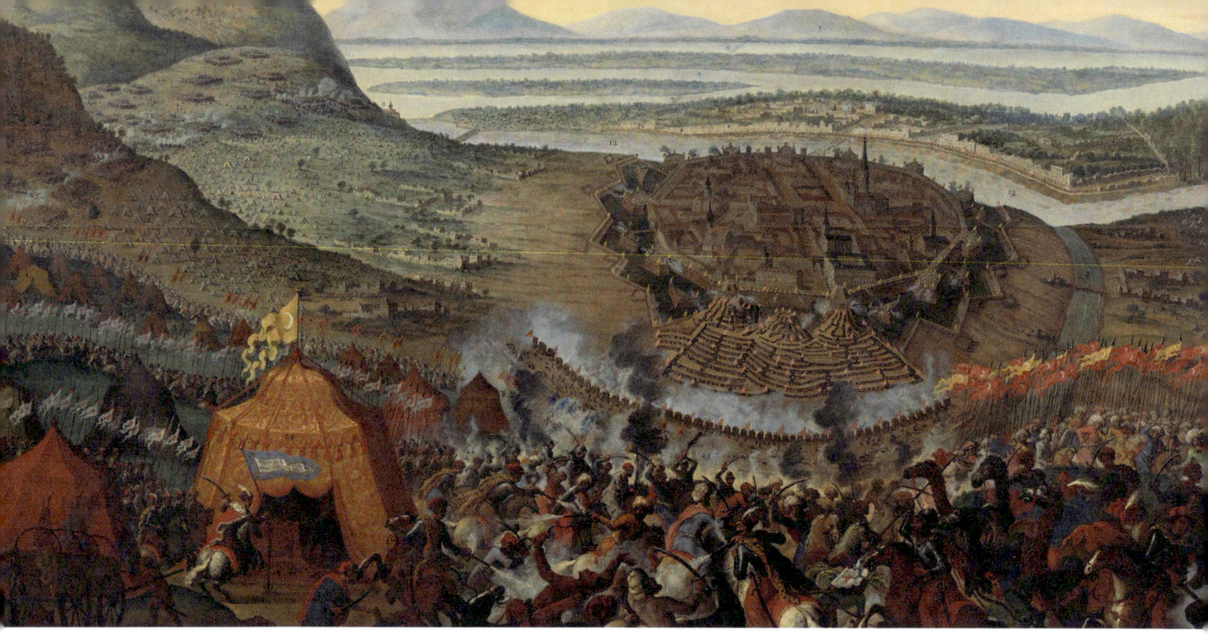

The Battle of Vienna (1683), painted by Frans Geffels between 1683 and 1694.

It was important for Willem that his ally Leopold I should be able to focus all his attention on the conflict with France. It was not to his advantage for the emperor to be embroiled in a war with the Ottomans at the same time. Willem therefore had to play a delicate diplomatic game. As stadtholder of the Republic and as king of England, he actively sought to promote peace between the two main warring parties, the sultan and the emperor. He was engaged in this effort in 1692 and 1693, the period when the mural on the Grand Staircase was completed. At that point, there was fierce fighting between France and the Grand Alliance under Willem's command. The war claimed many lives and cost vast sums, including for the Republic, so bringing an end to the Turkish war became a matter of even greater urgency.

Willem III wrote to Emperor Leopold on 23 July 1692 making it clear how difficult the situation was for him. He underlined the fact that he was embroiled in a gruelling conflict with France, both on land and at sea. Willem implored Leopold to consider his position, and urged him not to put the alliance under even greater pressure by fighting a war on two fronts. He warned that such a step would play into the hands of the enemy, the 'evil snake' Louis XIV.

Two days before writing his letter to Emperor Leopold, Willem had sent a message to the Ottoman sultan, Ahmed II. With great humility – as previously expressed to Leopold – he referred to his friendship and the mutual benefits of peace between the Ottomans and the Habsburgs. He let it be known that his

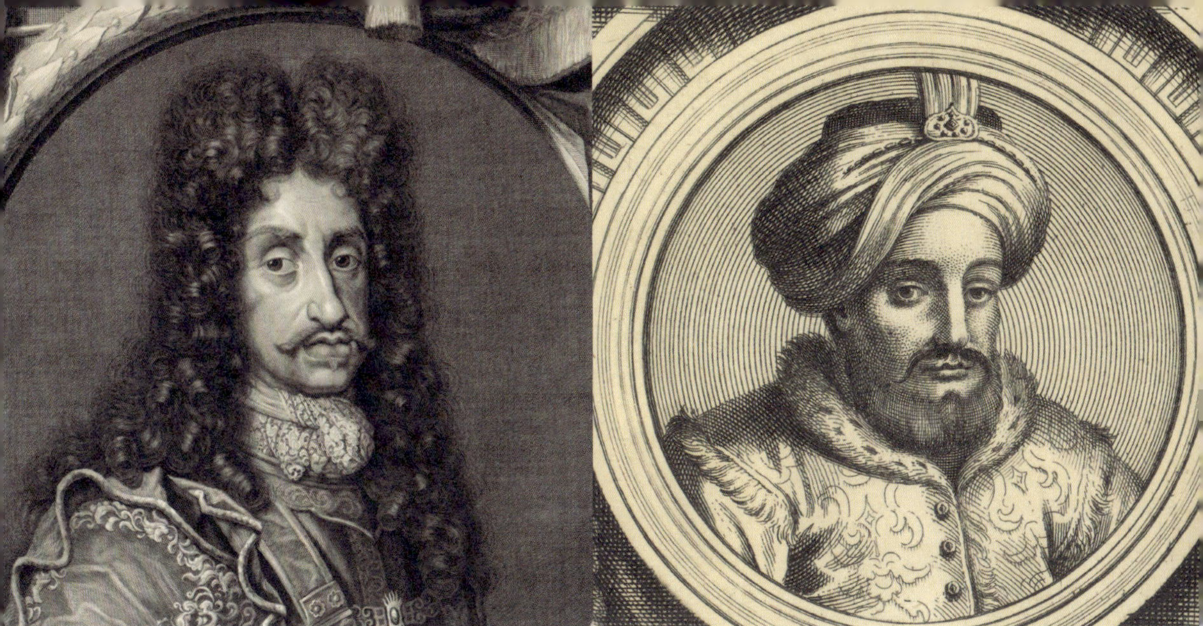

↑ **Habsburg Emperor Leopold I in an engraving by Pieter van Gunst, (detail).**

↗ **Posthumous portrait of sultan Ahmed II made by Nicolas Dorigny in 1699 (detail).**

attempt at mediation was intended 'to promote the Welfare and interests of the Ottoman Empire' and he signed the letter 'Your most affectionate Friend, William R[ex]'.

Willem and the sultan were not that close, of course. The tone was mainly a matter of the conventions of court etiquette. In an earlier letter to the Duke of Lorraine, Willem had expressed his delight at the duke's victory over the Turks at Esztergom in Hungary, in 1685. He had signed this letter 'Your Grace's most humble servant'.

As king of England and stadtholder of the Republic, Willem III ordered both a Dutch ambassador, Coenraad van Heemskerk (1646-1702), and an English ambassador, Lord William Paget (1637-1713), to work together at the court of Emperor Leopold in Vienna. Their mission: to lobby for peace with the Ottoman Empire.The same two ambassadors worked together a year later, in 1693, this time in Istanbul.

Your most affectionate Freind
William R.

Willem III signed his letter to sultan Ahmed II 'Your most affectionate Friend ['Freind']'.

A plea for peace

The depiction of current events – or allegories of such events – in murals was quite common in northern Europe at this time. Patrons were concerned not only with decorating the interior of their home, but were also often keen to make their political position clear and convincingly present an important message to visitors. The mural around the Grand Staircase can therefore be seen as a visual plea for peace between the Holy Roman Emperor and the Ottoman sultan. What is more, the painting emphasises Willem III's diplomatic role as a bridge builder between two worlds.

The landscape in the background looks most unlike the province of Gelderland. With its hills, water, castles, derelict forts and domed buildings, it is highly reminiscent of the Bosporus, the strait that passes through Istanbul, dividing the city between Europe and Asia. Highly distinctive, the Bosporus features in many 17th- and 18th-century views of Istanbul. One of the first examples in the Netherlands was a panorama almost ten metres in length that belonged to the collection of Grand Pensionary Adriaan Pauw (1585-1653). He displayed the spectacular print in his 'camer Constantinopelen' ('Constantinople Chamber')

Detail of a 1616/1617 etching by Pieter van der Keere depicting a panorama of Istanbul, which was probably lost when Heemstede Castle was demolished in 1810 (detail).

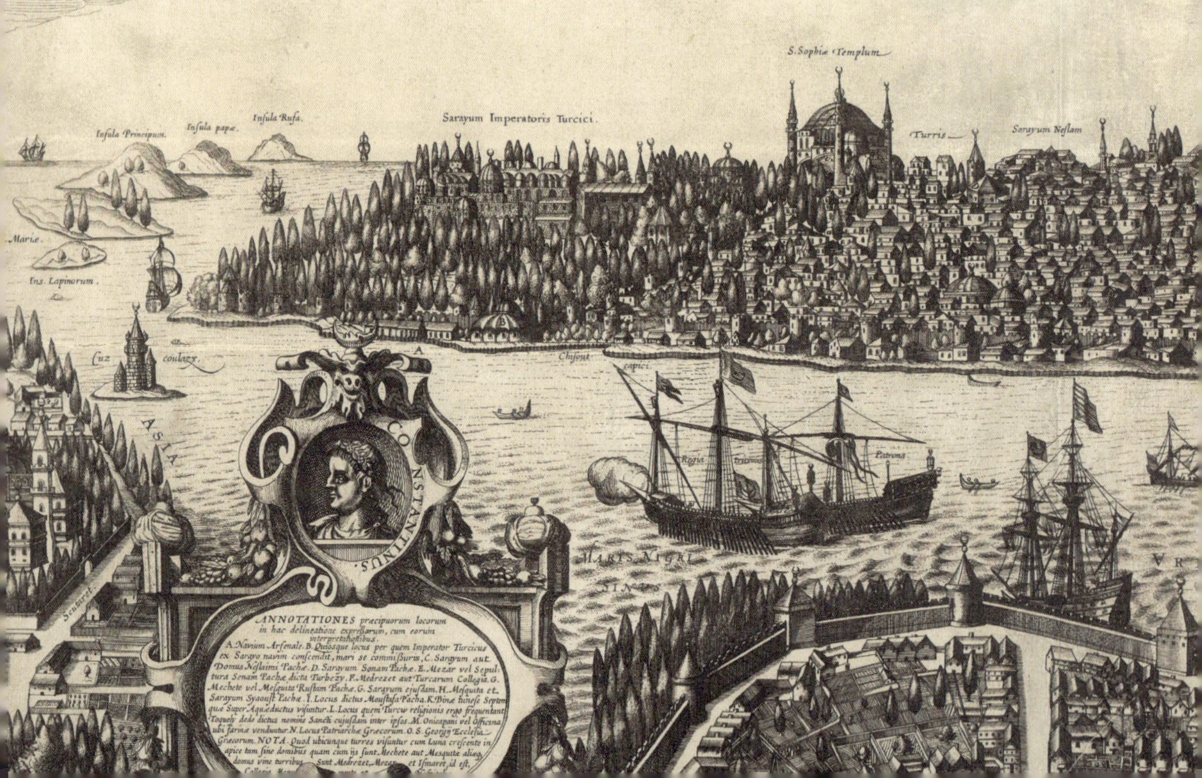

at Heemstede Castle. Vanmour also included the Bosporus in his views of the city, as seen from the Dutch embassy.

One striking feature of the background on the east wall of the staircase at Paleis Het Loo is a fortified tower. It might refer to the Rumelian Fortress. The historic fortress on the European banks of the Bosporus symbolised the Ottoman conquest of the city, when they took it from its former rulers, the Byzantines. The fortified tower and other ruins were probably not added to the mural until the 20th century, to underline the fact that it is the region around the Bosporus that is depicted in the painting.

With figures who seem to represent a high-ranking Ottoman delegation and a landscape resembling that beside the Bosporus in the background, the mural in Apeldoorn symbolises the meeting of Europe and Asia at Paleis Het Loo. It is a powerful visual representation of Willem's efforts to secure peace between the Holy Roman Empire and the Ottoman Empire. Since the decoration was also inspired by the Escalier des Ambassadeurs at Versailles, the image is not only a nod to Willem's role as a diplomatic mediator, but also a well-considered response to Louis XIV, a subtle message presenting Willem as a worthy rival to the Sun King.

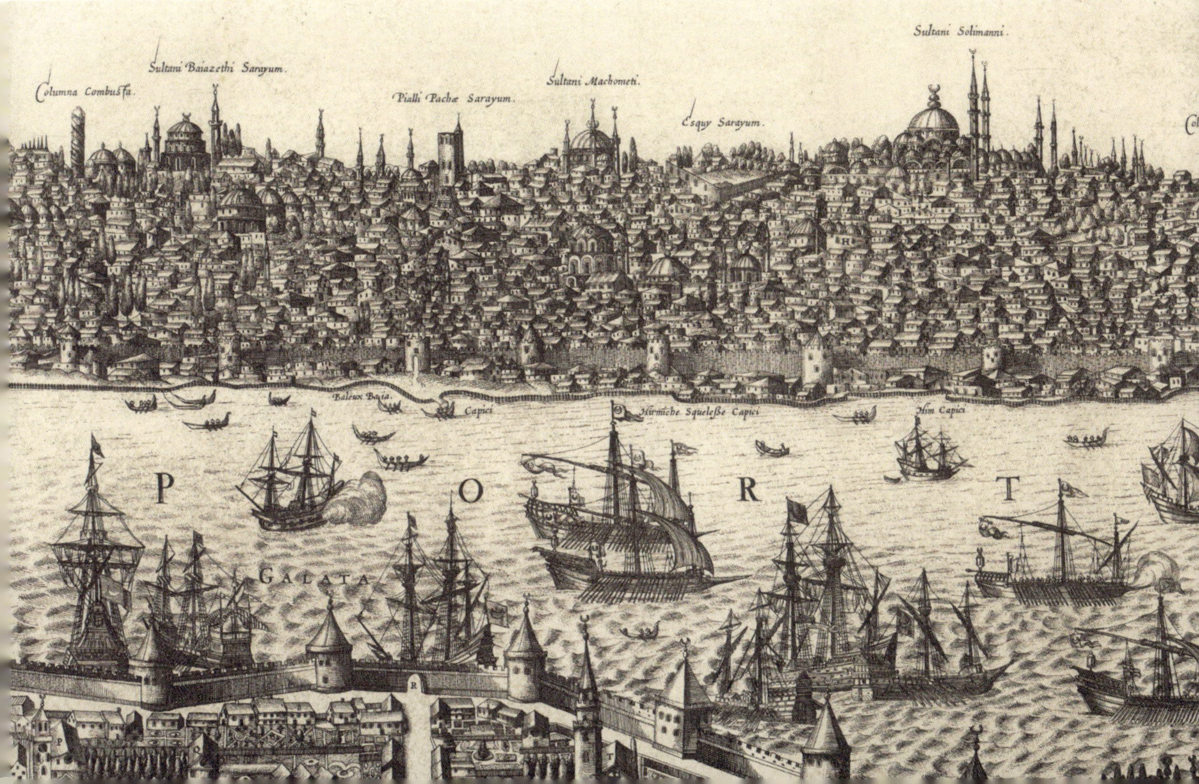

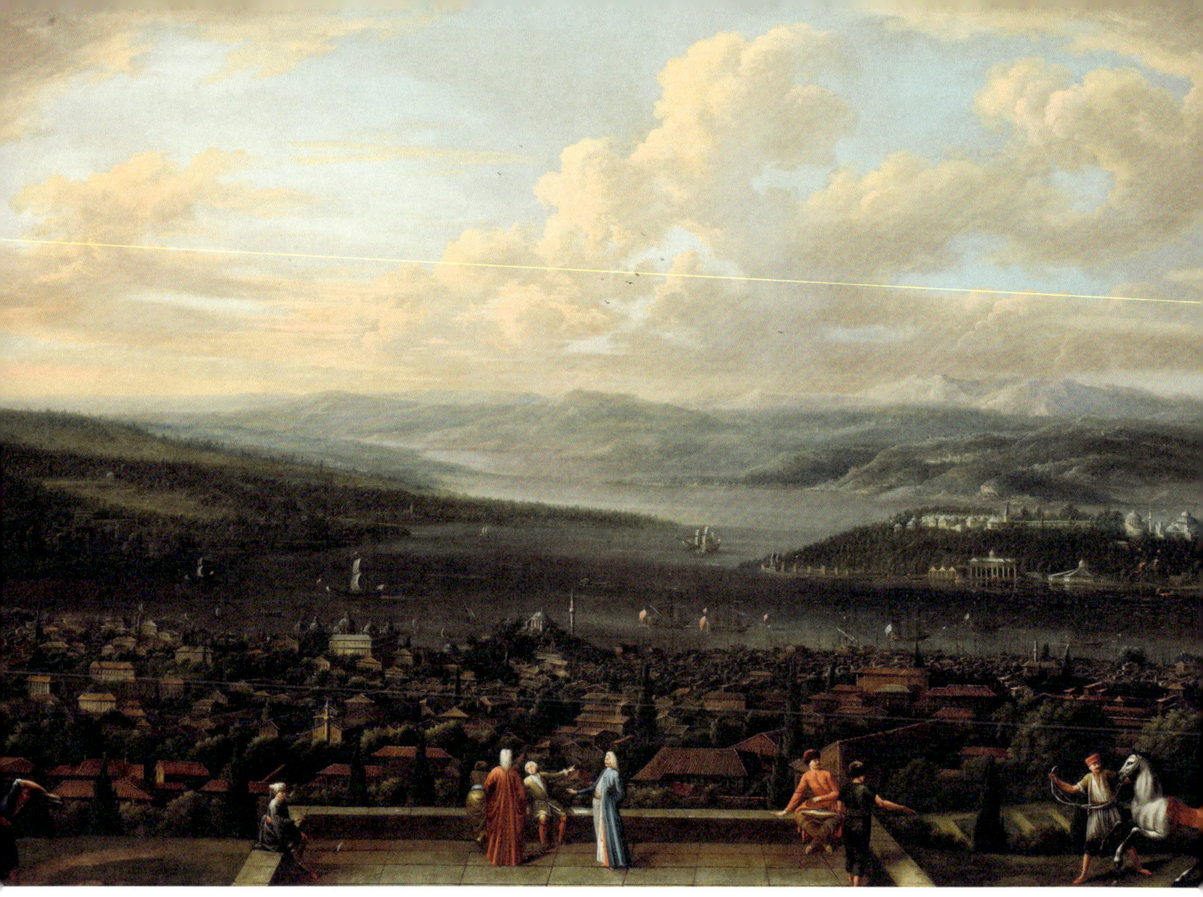

Vanmour painted this view of Istanbul from the Dutch embassy in the Pera neighbourhood between 1720 and 1737.

Willem knew that he could not outdo the splendour of Louis XIV's palace simply by imitating it, so he opted for another approach. Marot's design demonstrated that his ambition to outclass Louis was not a matter of brute military force, but of clever strategy and diplomacy. This message will have been clear to any diplomat who was received at Willem's summer palace. Anyone who attended an audience with the king-stadtholder would have to climb the staircase, and would be surrounded by the painting on the way in and out. Some years later, Willem took a similarly subtle approach with the mural for the King's Staircase at Hampton Court.

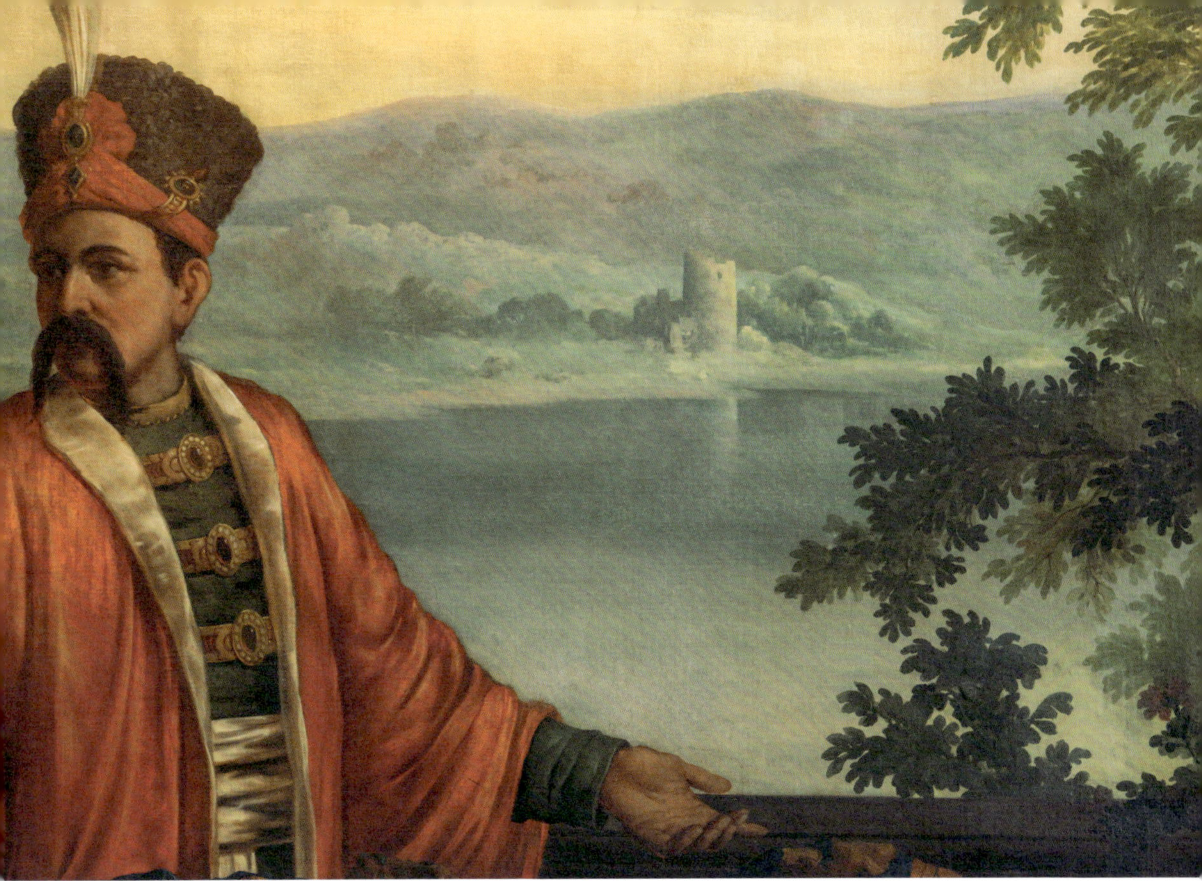

The fortress tower on the east wall.

Willem's diplomatic efforts were unsuccessful, and the Great Turkish War did not come to an end until the Treaty of Karlowitz was signed in 1699. By that time, Louis XIV posed less of a threat, as the Treaty of Rijswijk had already brought the Nine Years' War with France to an end in 1697. The painting on the Grand Staircase can be seen as a unique historical record of this turbulent period. These events steadily receded into the background after Willem's death in 1702 and, since the original meaning of the mural had never been documented, it was gradually forgotten.

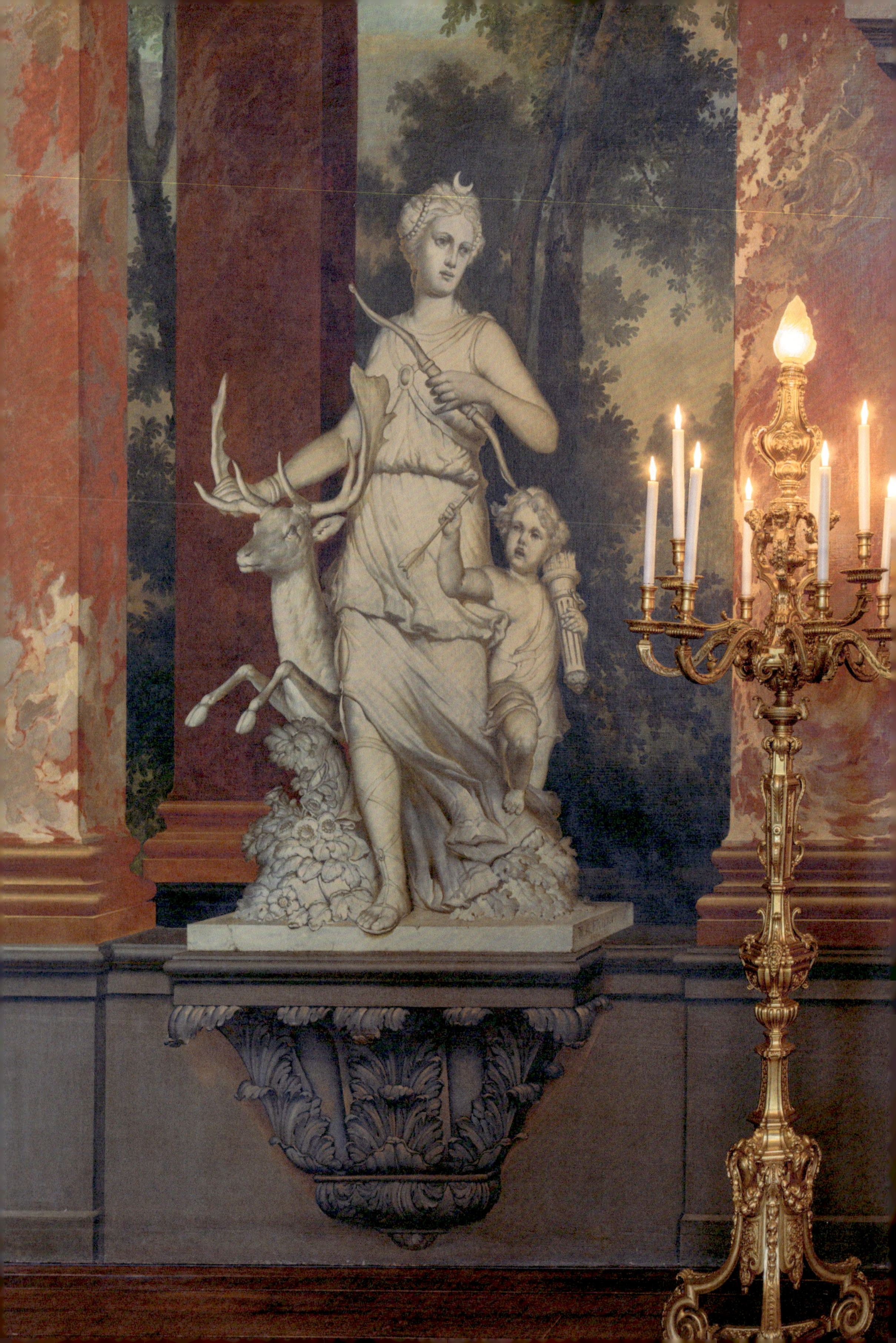

Metamorphosis

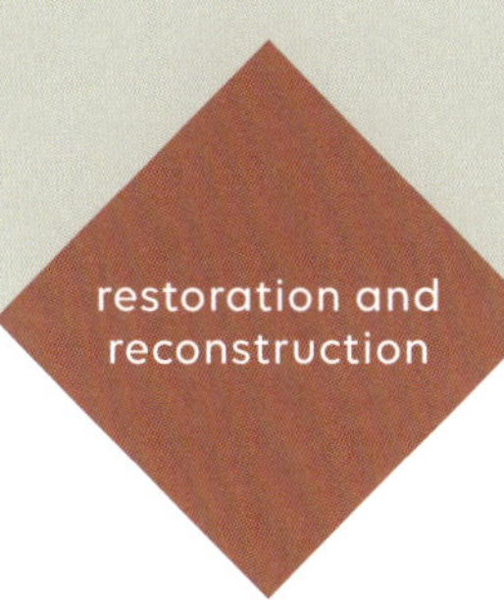

Through the centuries, the mural on the Grand Staircase at Paleis Het Loo has undergone changes both big and small. Court painter Jan van Dijk (c. 1690-1769) carried out the first restoration between 1728 and 1737, when the painting was only just over a quarter of a century old. Robbert Duval may have used walnut oil in his varnish, leading to rapid discoloration and even damage to the paint. Another possibility is that the wall was not dry enough when the oil paint was applied, so it soon began to flake off. We do not know whether Van Dijk adapted the original design. No evidence has yet been found of what his restoration entailed, or what may have happened to the mural during the rest of the 18th century.

Covered with white plaster

The Netherlands was under French rule from 1795 to 1813. The painting was in poor condition once more when Louis Napoleon ascended the Dutch throne in 1806. Furthermore, murals had fallen out of fashion by now. This was the era of neoclassicism in art and architecture, when architects were inspired by the ideals of the ancient Greeks and Romans. Symmetry and clean lines were paramount. Natural stone and plasterwork were important architectural materials. The lavish baroque decoration at Paleis Het Loo was regarded

← Diana, Roman goddess of the hunt, by the door to the Great Hall.

↓ The back of the palace and the garden following the renovation during the period of French rule, painted by Andreas Schelfhout in 1838, (p. 64-65).

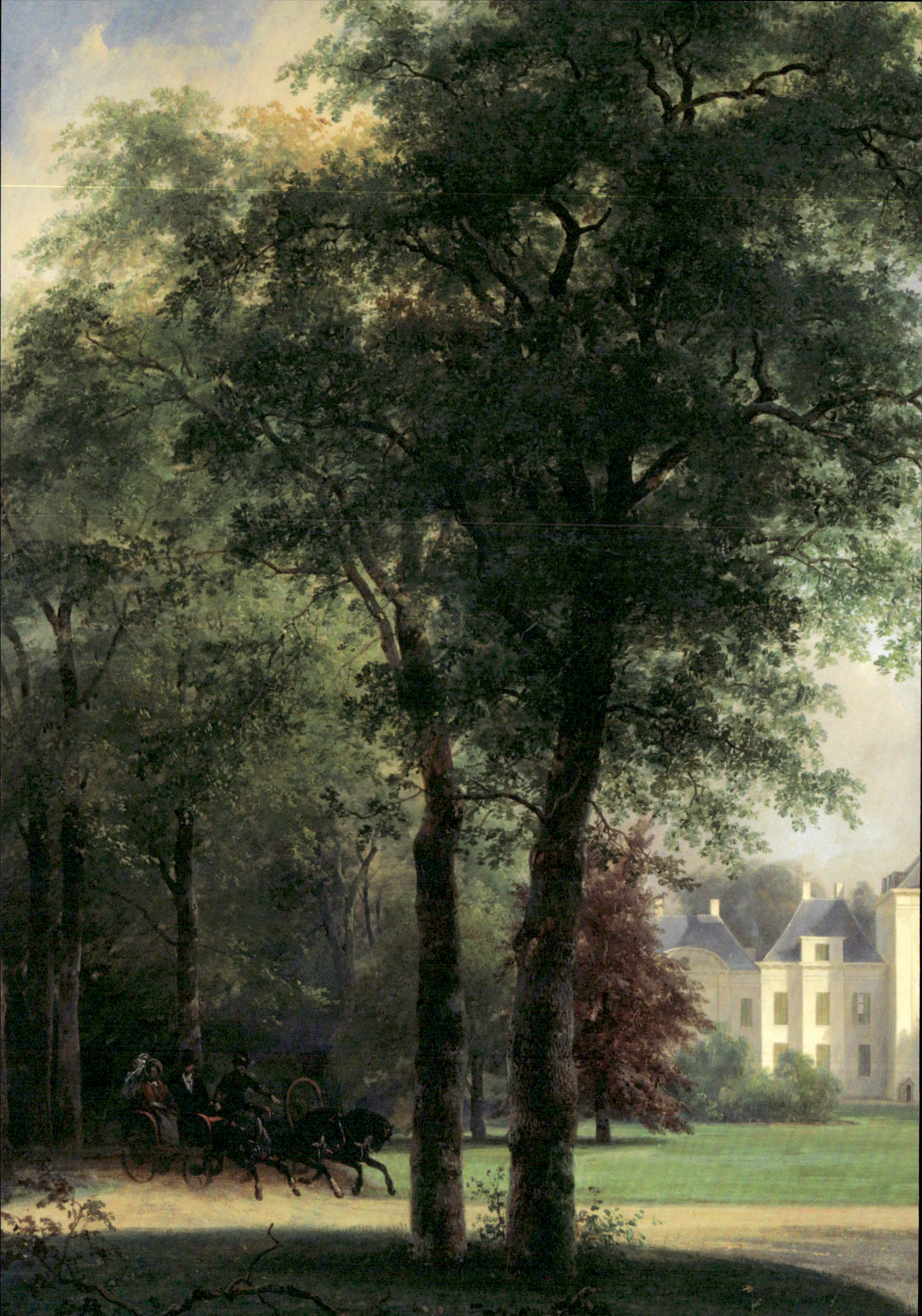

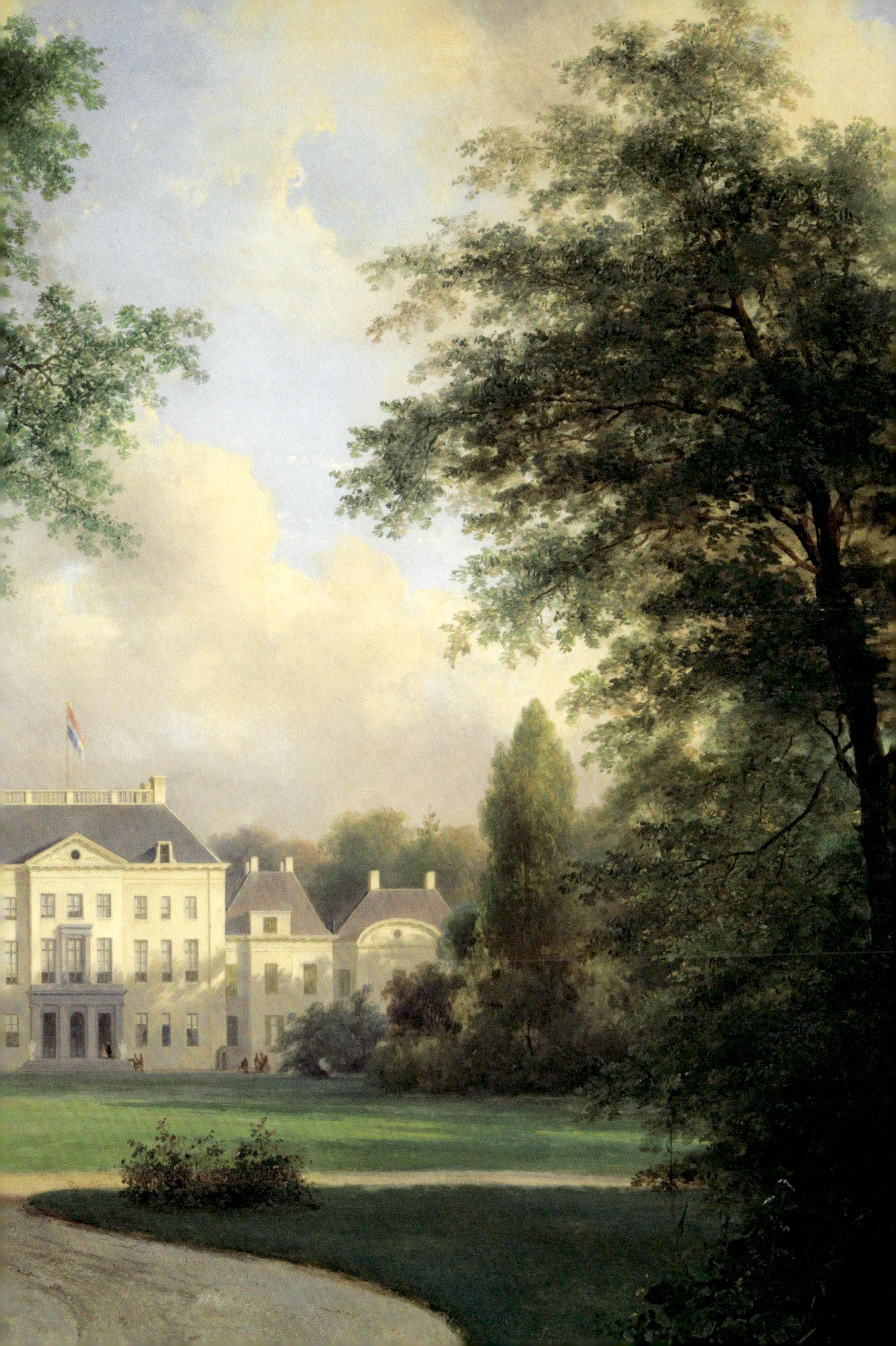

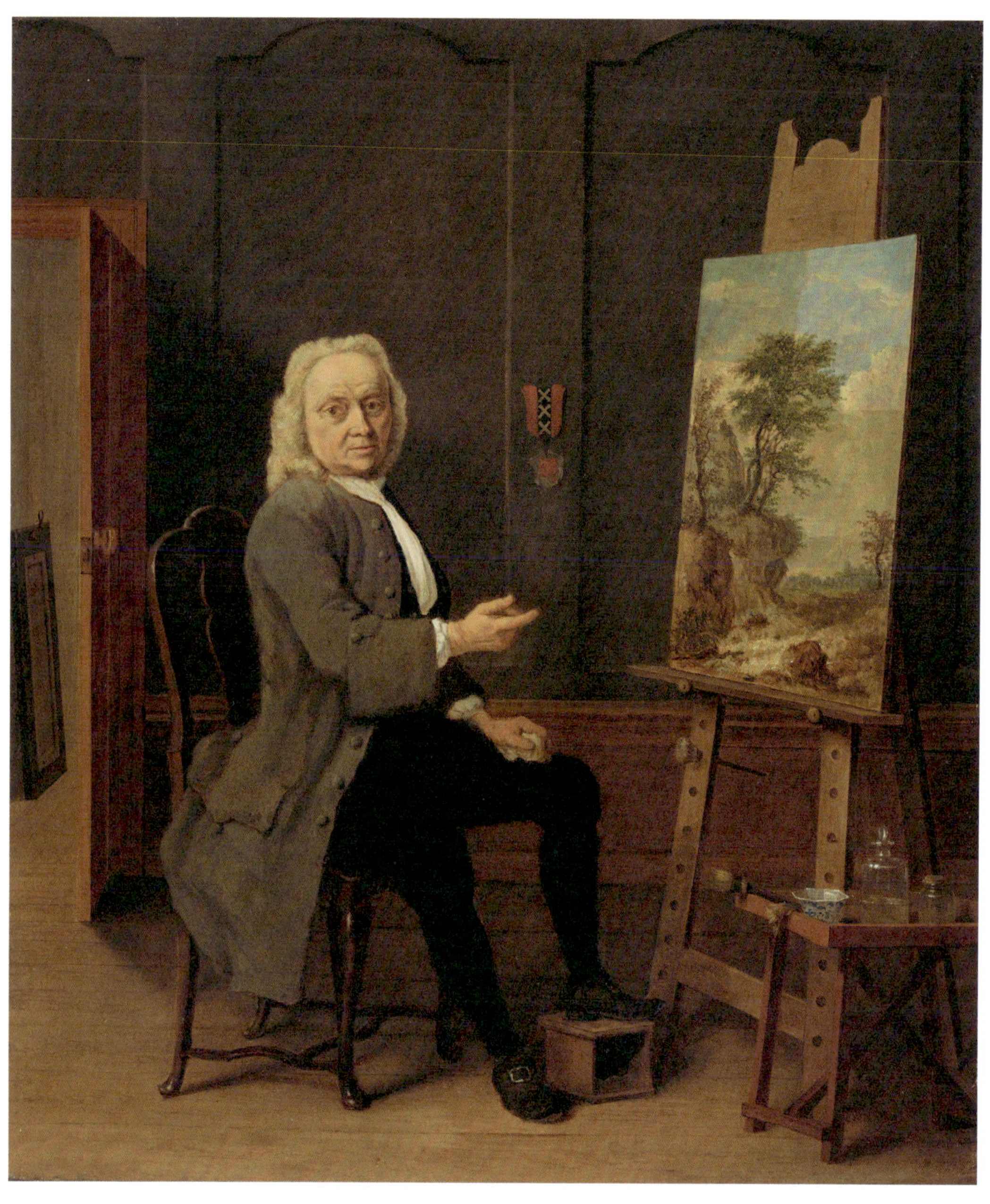

Court painter Jan van Dijk restoring a painting, portrayed in 1754 by Jan ten Compe.

as old-fashioned. Since the palace was to become the French king's summer residence, a thorough renovation of the building was ordered, from the façade and interiors to the gardens. The brick façades and the walls of the staircase were rendered with white plaster.

The work probably started after 14 February 1807, when eighteen house painters were first recorded as working at Paleis Het Loo. It proceeded very rapidly. The ceiling was finished on 29 April and the scaffolding up the Grand Staircase had been removed by the beginning of May. Since there are no pictures of the staircase in this period, we do not know whether any form of decoration was added to the white walls.

Louis Napoleon was able to enjoy his newly modernised palace for only a short time, as he had to leave the Netherlands after just four years. King Willem I, the oldest son of Stadtholder Willem V, was appointed in 1815. He used Paleis Het Loo as a summer palace, and did nothing to reverse the changes made by the French. His son, King Willem II, also left the palace as it was.

The staircase at the time of Willem III

King Willem III's investiture took place in 1849. We know more about what the staircase looked like during his reign. A restoration report tells us that in 1850 the 'walls beside the staircase' were painted. This probably refers to the walls on either side of the stairs up to the first landing. In 1874 the walls – probably those from the first landing up – were covered with marbled paper. Paper was also applied to the flat and vaulted ceilings. The east and west walls were painted a sandstone colour, covered in brown jute, and decorated with a display of weapons, banners and other military trophies. Two paintings by Javanese artist Raden Saleh (1807-1880) were also hung there. A white stucco cornice was affixed some two metres below the ceiling.

Parts of the original 17th-century paintwork were discovered for the first time in 1888. The king had his staff investigate whether the original decoration was still present, using Marot's print as a guide. Parts of the painting were revealed when plaster was chipped away on a side wall. Subsequently, the other walls were also examined.

Changes under a young queen

Despite these finds, the staircase remained in the same state until Queen Wilhelmina (1880-1962) acceded the throne in 1898. Partly out of admiration for her predecessors from the stadtholder era – particularly King-Stadtholder Willem III – and partly from an aversion to her parents' taste in decoration, she had the palace returned to its original 17th-century baroque style, using examples of Marot's work as a basis.

The renovation work started in the vestibule, the palace's entrance hall. Several parties were involved, including architect Johannes Jacobus van Nieukerken (1854-1913), the intendant of Paleis Het Loo Joan A. van Steyn (1855-1926), responsible for the management of Paleis Het Loo, Rotterdam furniture manufacturer C.H. Eckhart and decorative painter Willem Fabri. The restoration of the vestibule turned out to be a complex undertaking.

Architect Van Nieukerken was appointed to oversee the project, but eventually attempted to expand his brief, as he was keen to restore the staircase. The matter was discussed in late October 1898 and Van Nieukerken started measuring up both the vestibule and the staircase in early November. He drew up a budget and produced design drawings on his own initiative, visiting the Royal Library and the National Archive and Binnenhof parliament building for inspiration. The ceiling in particular was inspired by the Trêveszaal (Truce Hall), which Marot had designed later in his career. The Trêveszaal has a painted circular opening surrounded by cartouches in grey tones, similar to that in Marot's print of Paleis Het Loo. Van Nieukerken also looked to Pieter Post's ceiling in the Senate chamber, with figures painted by Duval's mentor Nicolaas Wielingh. Together with Marot's print of the staircase in Apeldoorn, these examples gave Van Nieukerken all the building blocks he needed, and on 10 November he presented his plans to the intendant, Joan A. van Steyn.

After the queen had seen his sketches, scaffolding was erected along the staircase. Work to remove the marbled paper and the top layer of plaster on the walls commenced in mid-November. After the paper had been removed, remains of the painted reliefs were discovered, surrounded by gold oak leaves. When the stucco cornice was also removed, the original painted cornice was revealed. The first remnants of Duval's painting were uncovered on the west wall on 16 November.

→ **Thérèse Schwartze (1851-1918) portrayed Queen Wilhelmina to mark her investiture in September 1898.**

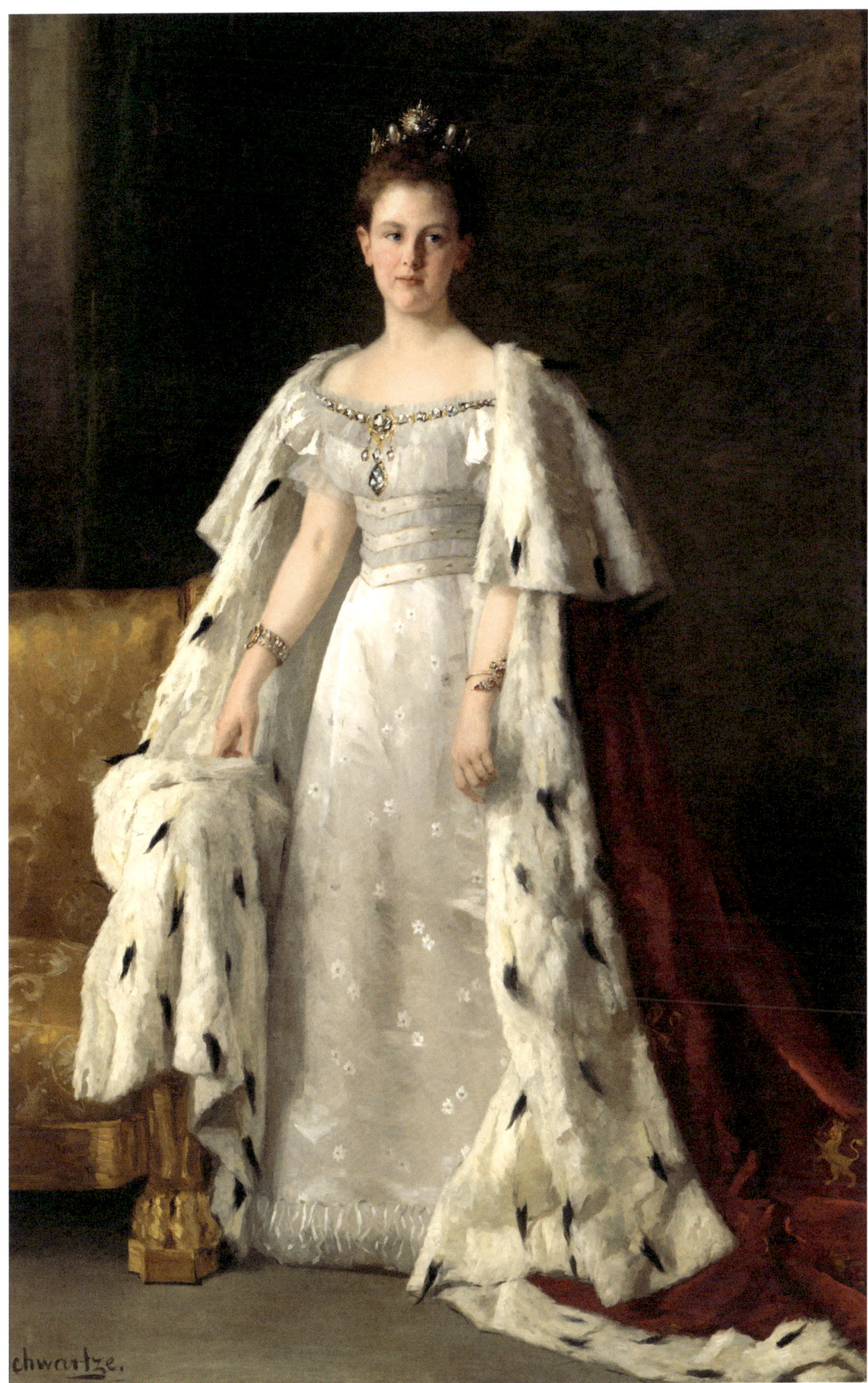
chwartze.

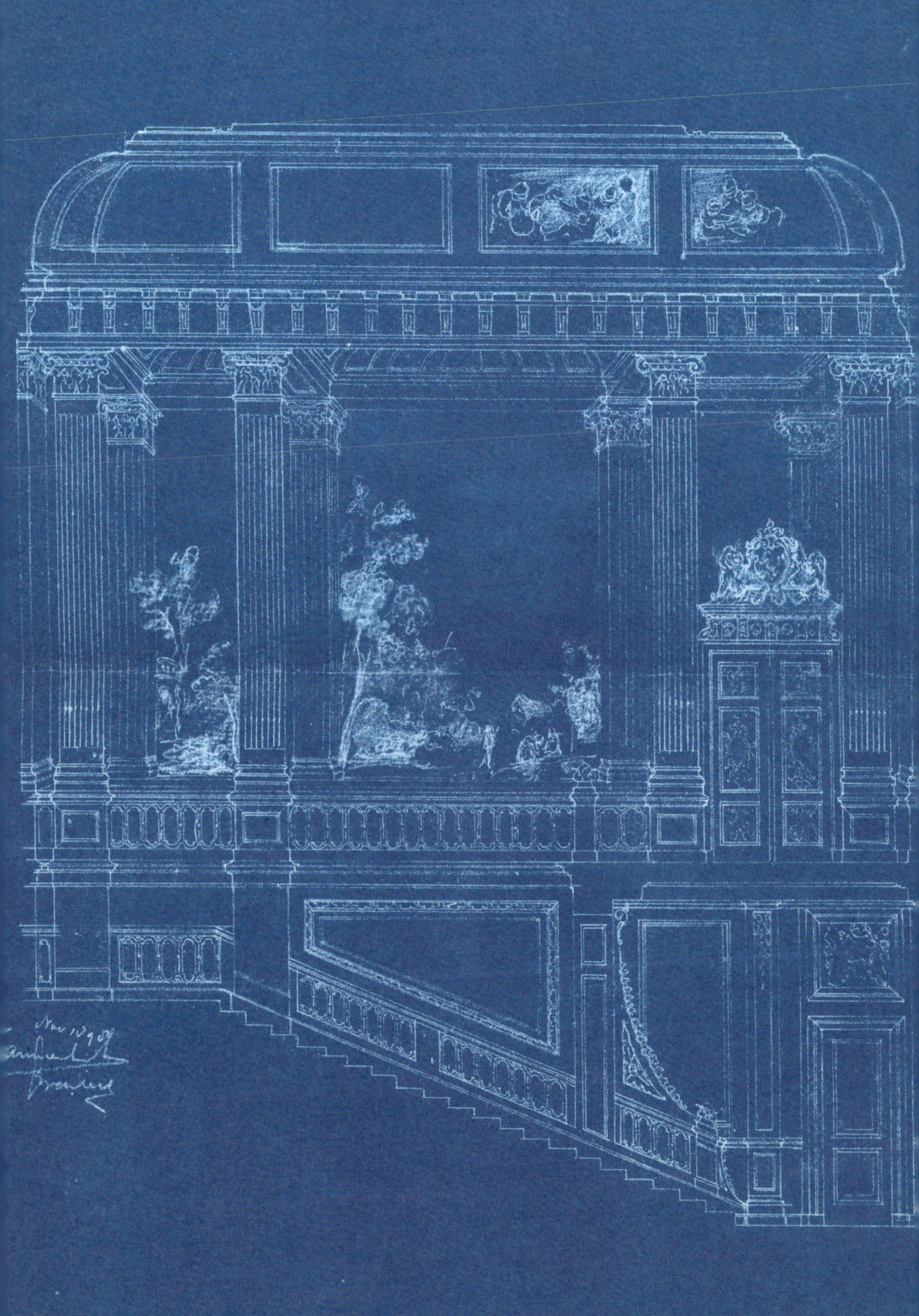

When a tack was removed from the covering so that it could be replaced, a piece of painted plaster flew off the wall, unexpectedly revealing a fragment of a man's head in the 17th-cenury mural. Wilhelmina's mother Emma (1858-1934), who was staying at the palace at the time, immediately ordered the weapon trophies to be moved to the art gallery, and had tests carried out in several places to see whether more of Marot's design had survived. A second man's head was uncovered. By the end of November, the plaster had been removed from the entire west wall, including the sections between the windows and part of the ceiling.

Architect Van Nieukerken proposed that the remains of the mural not be restored immediately, in order to preserve the original work. He also doubted whether further additions would survive. Over the centuries, the paintwork had had to withstand a great deal, and he believed a large proportion had already been overpainted. He therefore suggested that the design be copied onto canvas, which would then be mounted on the wall. Strangely, however, despite his own advice, the architect could not resist coming up with possible designs to fill in the missing parts. As a quick pencil sketch of the fragments revealed, presumably by Van Nieukerken, the empty spaces were even to be filled with mules.

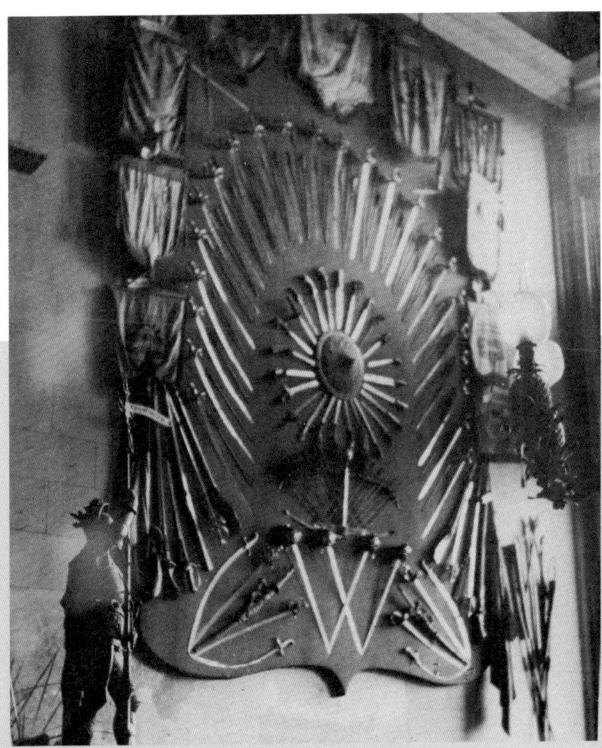

← Blueprint of a design that Van Nieukerken and his son made for the east wall.

→ The west wall with King Willem III's display of weapons and crests.

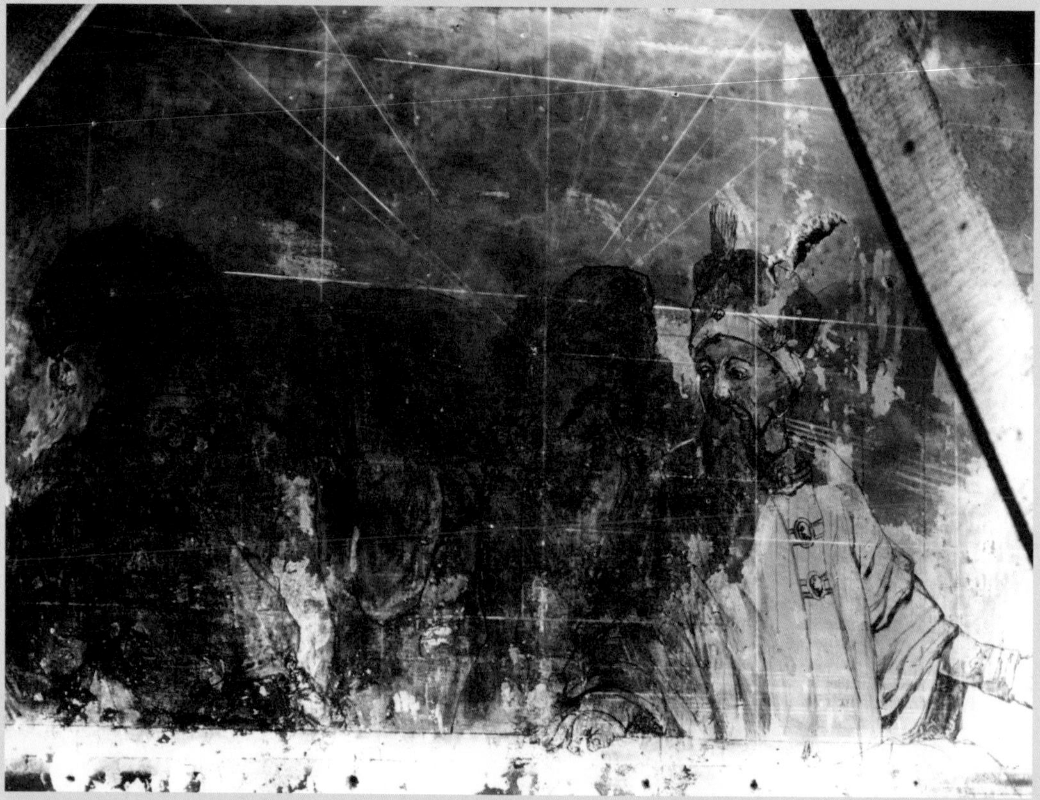

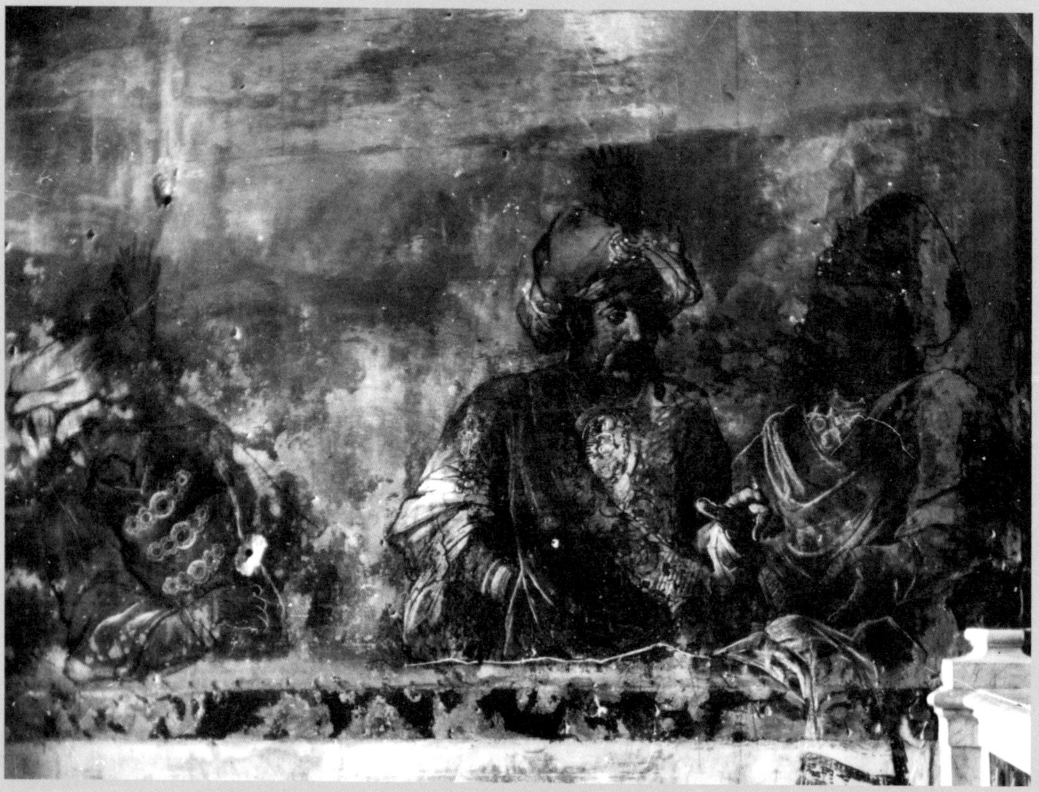

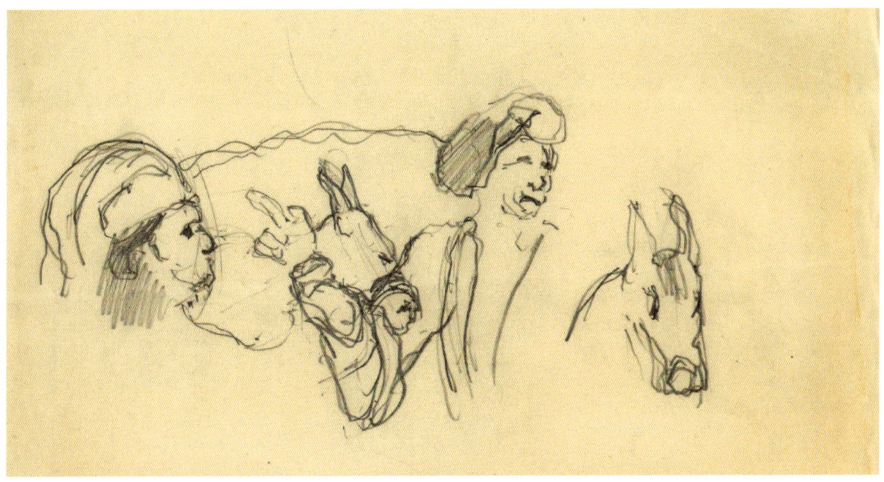

With mules as an 'Middle Eastern' addition, Van Nieukerken presumably sought to emphasise that the figures are not individuals, but 'oriental characters' from an ancient painting tradition.

Willem Fabri's restoration

Ultimately, Van Nieukerken was not commissioned to restore the staircase. In early 1899, Wilhelmina decided to award the commission to painter Willem Fabri of Rotterdam, who would perform the work with his assistants A. Albers, H.G. Luitwieler, K. Hoogendorp and H.P. Groen.

Various ideas were put forward as to how the empty or damaged areas might be filled. There was for example a proposal to incorporate the mottos of Wilhelmina's ancestors into the painting. But little progress was made on the restoration work for a year, as efforts focused on the completion of the vestibule. It was not until April 1900 that Fabri and his team started to carefully examine the staircase. This examination, which involved scraping all of the covering layer of plaster and paint from the walls and ceiling, took until the end of July. Fabri made an oil sketch to scale of the west wall, which he presented to Queen Wilhelmina for approval.

↖ The first figures to be revealed during the restoration work were the ones on the west wall.

← Remains of the painting were also found on the east wall in 1898.

↓ Willem Fabri (on the right, dressed in a suit) and his team pose in front of the reconstructed mural, September 1902 (p. 74-75).

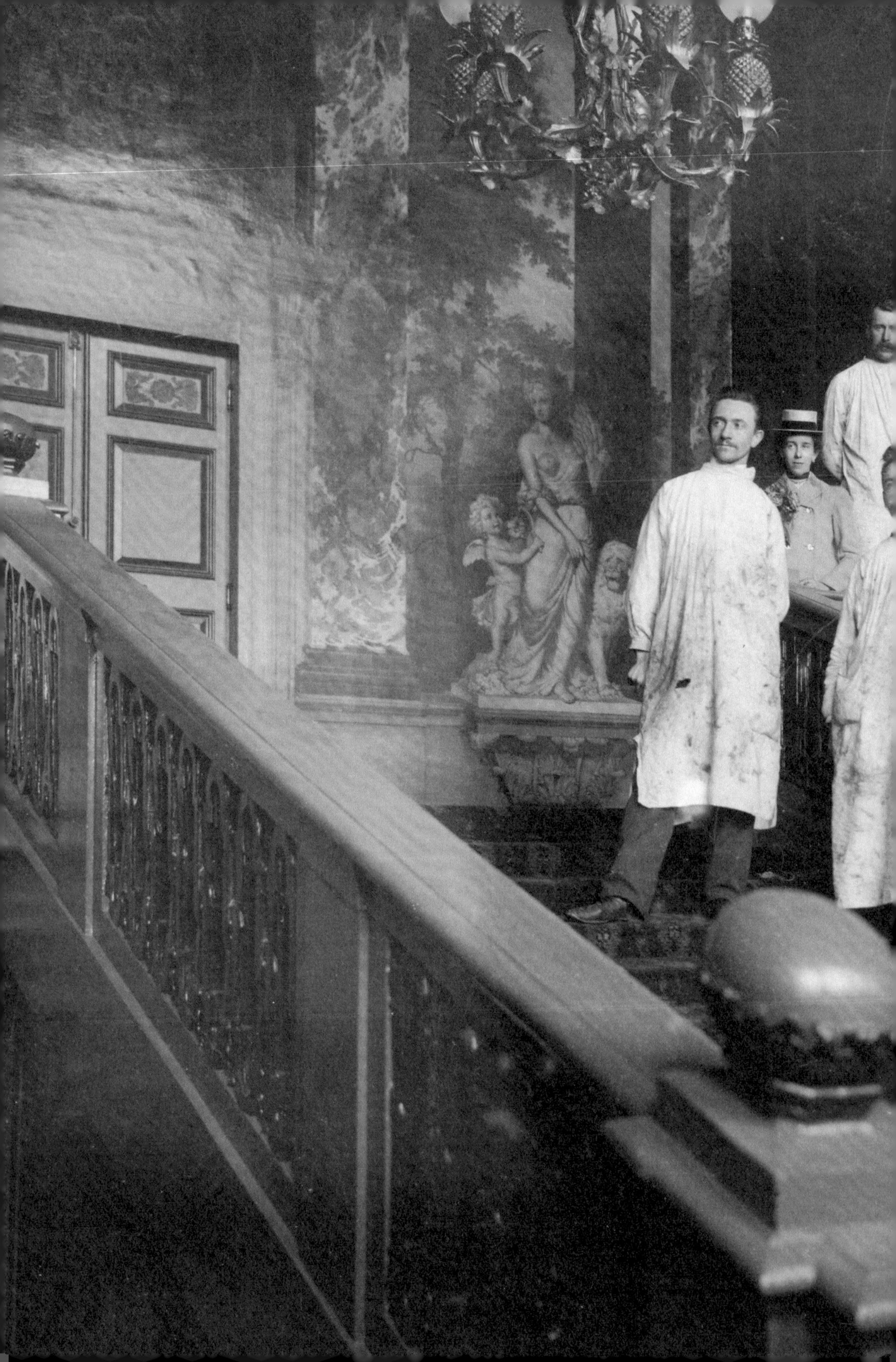

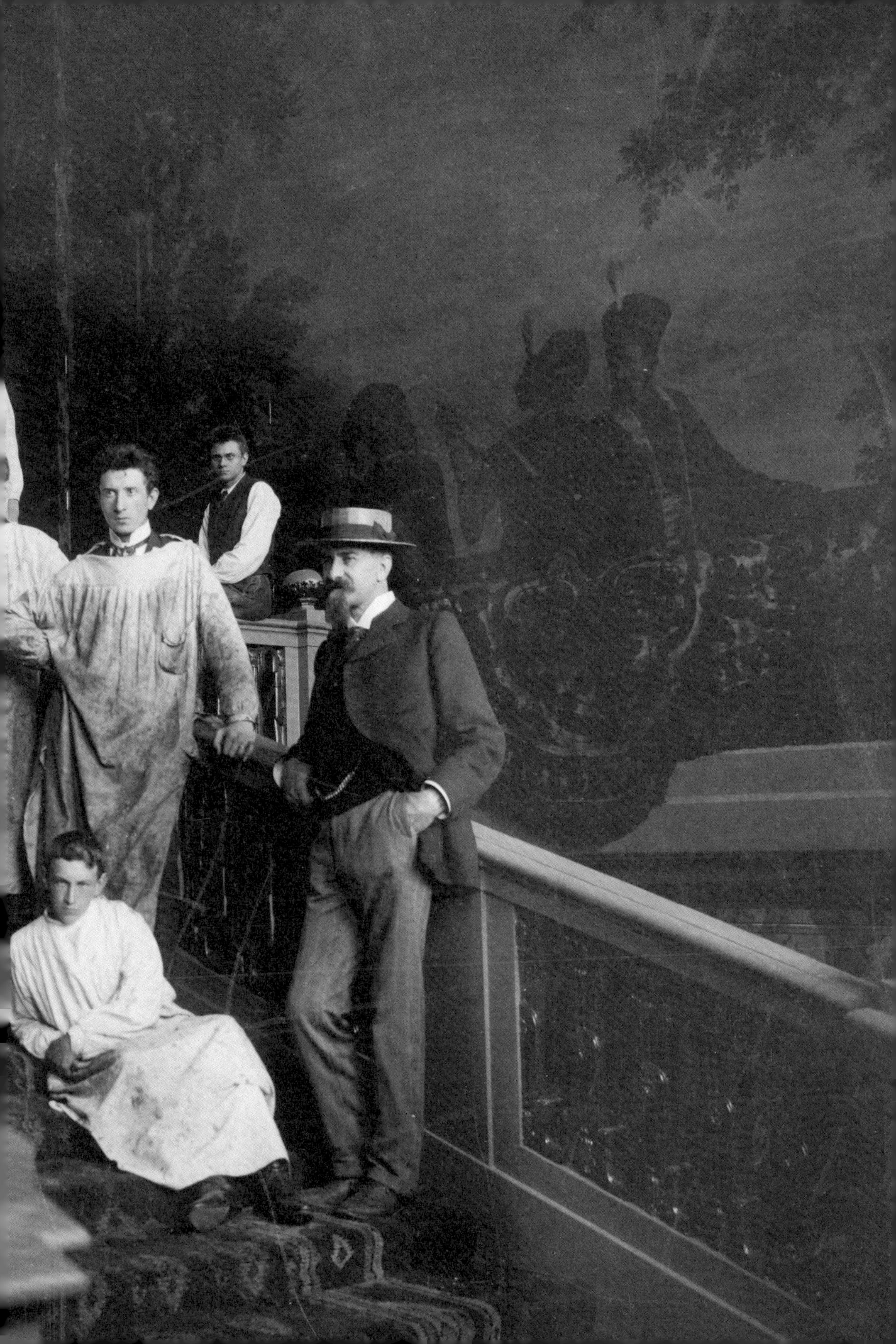

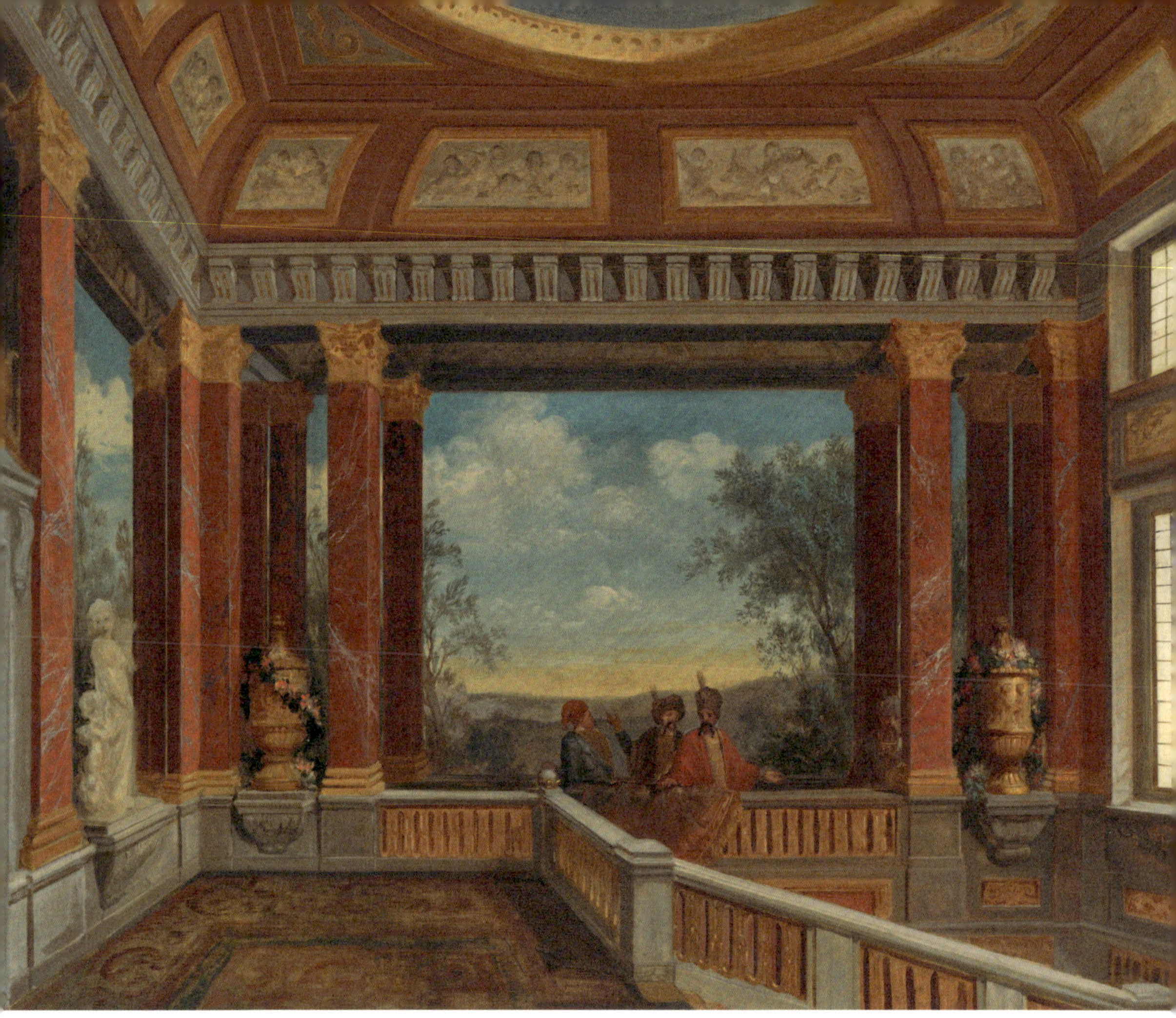

Fabri made this oil study on canvas to show the queen how the restored west wall would look.

After receiving the queen's approval, he had the image drawn out in its true size. The top plaster layer on the ceiling was removed and replaced with a new layer of lime shell where necessary. The covering on the walls and ceiling could thus be reapplied without the staircase having to be closed while the canvases were painted in Fabri's workshop. The outlines in the exposed painting that had sustained damage were traced and measurements taken, and the best-preserved coloured fragments were carefully covered with linen and removed from the wall. They were taken to Fabri's studio in Rotterdam to serve as a guide for the restoration, allowing the painters to adhere as closely as possible to the original colours and motif. These fragments, which were to be returned to the palace after use, have presumably been lost. The walls of the staircase were again covered with temporary canvas, on which portraits of Wilhelmina's ancestors and the young queen herself were hung. Guests were still being received at the palace, and they had to climb the staircase in order to attend their audience with the queen.

All remained quiet on the staircase for another year, while Fabri and his assistants carefully copied the paintings onto canvas in their workshop. They were probably almost finished in the summer of 1901, as Fabri requested in July that the staircase be made available from early December. At around the same time, the firm Eckhart wished to start with the carpentry work on the staircase. Two doors and their frames on either side of the Great Hall were to be replaced by concealed doors, so that the painting could continue across them.

Once the ceiling and walls had been made flush in early 1902, the painted canvases could be mounted. The ceiling consisted of a single huge canvas measuring fourteen by six metres. Eckhart completed the carpentry work in June, and the canvases were in place by the end of August. It was now time for the finishing touches. A Deventer carpet in the style of a Turkish Smyrna rug was laid on the stairs, to replace a similar carpet that had lain there before. The staircase was completed in late September 1902. The restoration of the murals had cost 26,000 guilders, a huge sum at that time.

Creative solutions

The rediscovered remains showed that Duval had not precisely followed the design in Marot's print when painting the staircase. He made the figures more vigorous by making small changes to their posture and gestures. Marot may have deliberately kept his design sketchy so that Duval could give it his own interpretation.

Fabri revitalised the 17th-century decorations. Where traces of Marot's design were still visible, his work closely followed them. But where time had erased those traces, he used his own creativity. Fabri made some conspicuous changes on the east wall. The figure on the left once held a poppy in his hand and had a striking moustache. Fabri turned the poppy into a peony and omitted the moustache. He also softened the look of the central figure.

Fabri barely had any original 17th-century images to fall back on for the north and south walls, so he had to improvise more there. A number of ideas were proposed, including by carpentry firm Eckhart. Eventually, Fabri painted mythological sculptures on the south wall, with Willem and Mary's coat of arms above the door to the Great Hall, as seen in Marot's print.

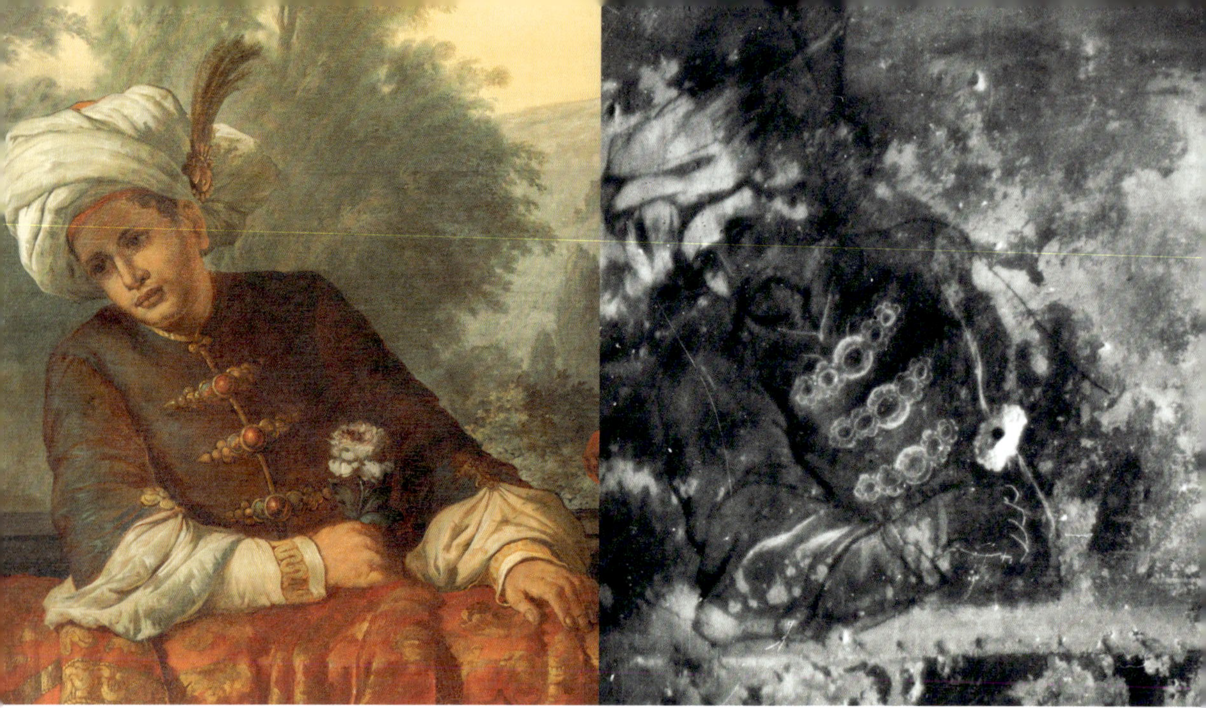

The figure on the left lost the moustache he had in the original Duval version, and Fabri turned the poppy in his hand into a peony.

There are no surviving detailed designs by Marot for the sculptures of Roman goddesses beside the door to the Great Hall. Only the distinctive crescent moon remained of the figure on the left, representing goddess of the hunt Diana, a small clue that assisted the restoration team. Other than that, they were forced to improvise.

Fabri adapted Marot's sketchy design as it appears in the 17th-century print. He drew inspiration for the Diana statue from a famous classical example, the 'Diana of Versailles'. And so, she remained recognisable in the painting as goddess of the hunt and thus symbolic of the palace's original function. To the right of the door to the Great Hall, the partially recovered figure of the goddess of fruitful abundance, Pomona, was replaced by Ceres, goddess of agriculture, the harvest and fertility.

Even Victor de Stuers (1843–1916), the founder of heritage management in the Netherlands, became involved in the restoration, though his role was probably mainly advisory. His notes reveal that he had proposed in 1898 that Willem and Mary's coat of arms be painted above the door to the Great Hall. Only part of the crest was schematically indicated in Marot's print. Fabri followed De Stuers' advice.

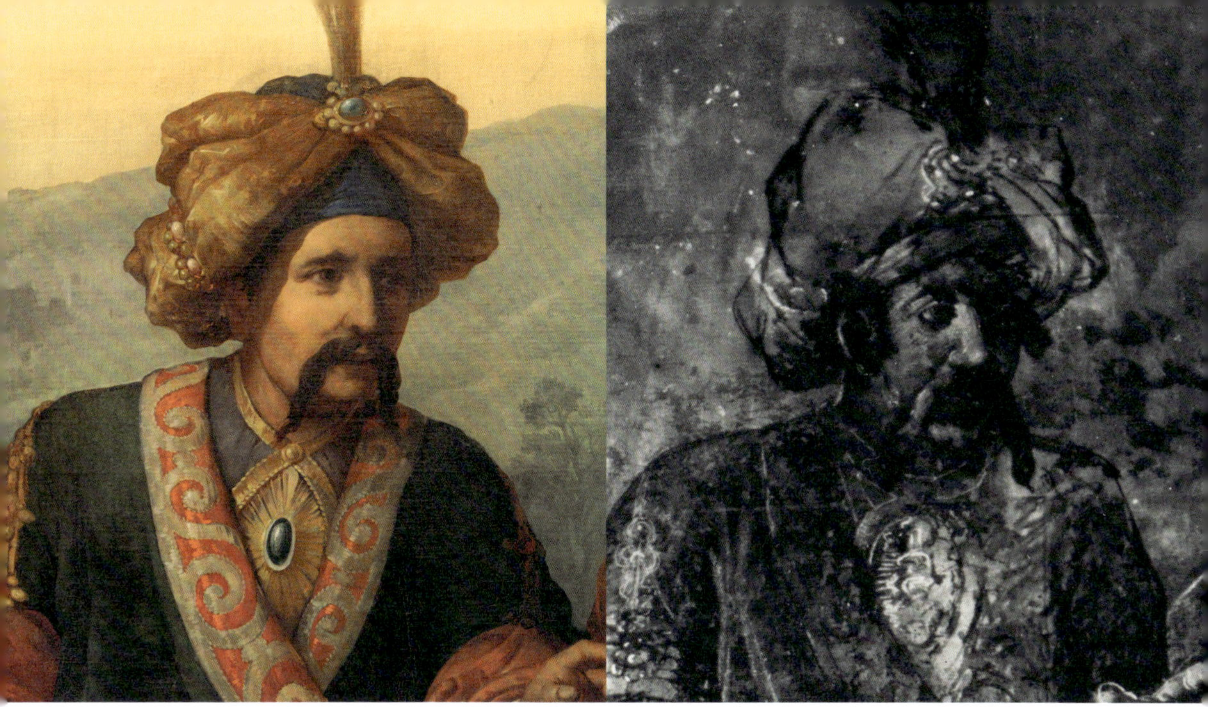

↑ The facial features of the central figure on the east wall are less pronounced than in the remains of the original.

↓ Carpentry firm Eckhart presented this sketch for the north and south walls.

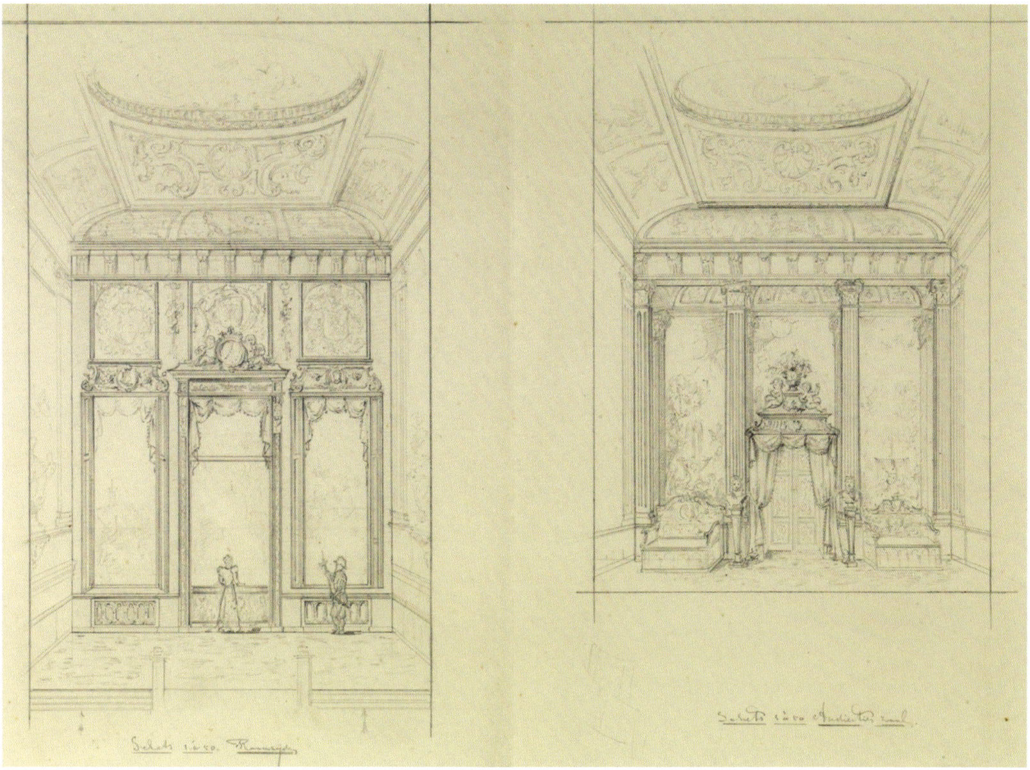

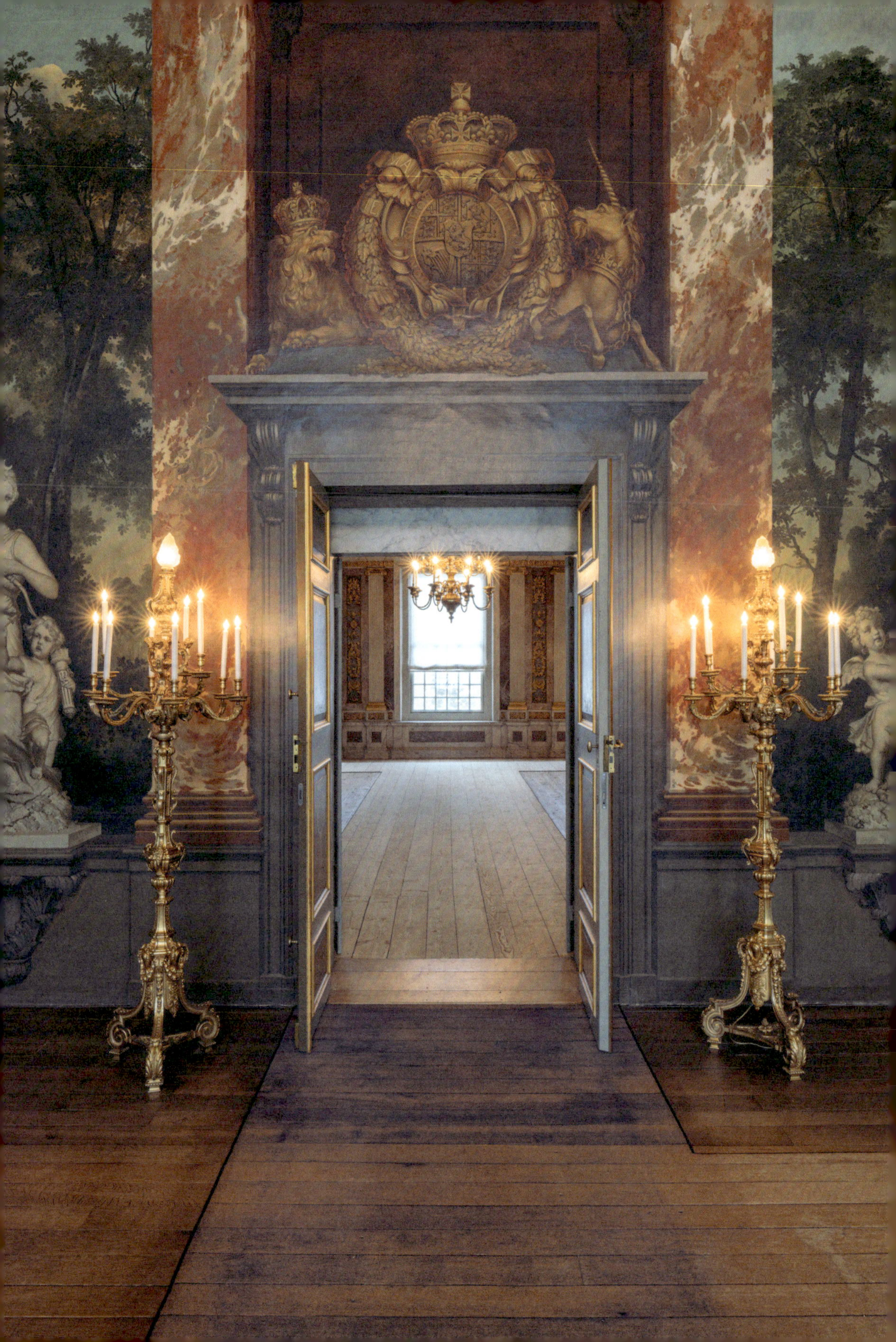

No remains of the original painting were found on the north wall, and Marot's print did not provide any basis for the restoration. Fabri covered most of the wall with decorative motifs and allowed daylight to enter through the six windows. He deviated from the overall 17th-century concept here. There is no dialogue between the side walls and the north wall, which instead presents a visual summary of the 19th-century history of the staircase. The shields, armour and weapons on the painted pilasters beside the central window recall the time when such items were hung on the walls of the staircase. Above the other windows there are cartouches with symbols of the hunt, and between them there is a medallion with a portrait of the young Queen Wilhelmina in the guise of the goddess Diana, with the crescent moon on her head.

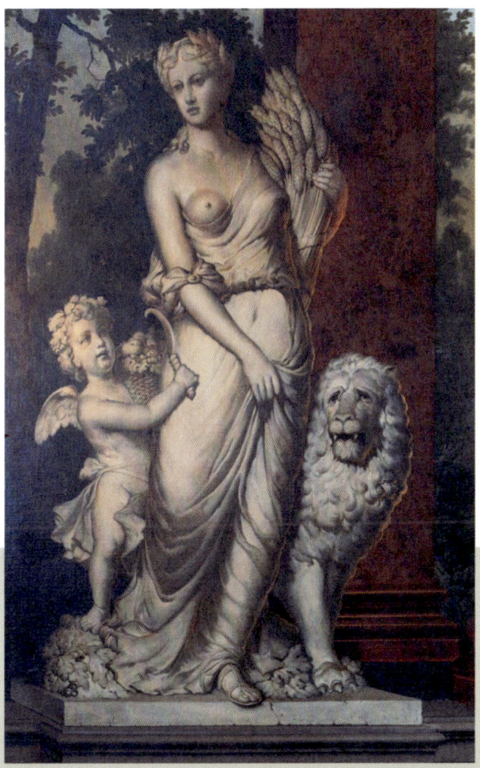

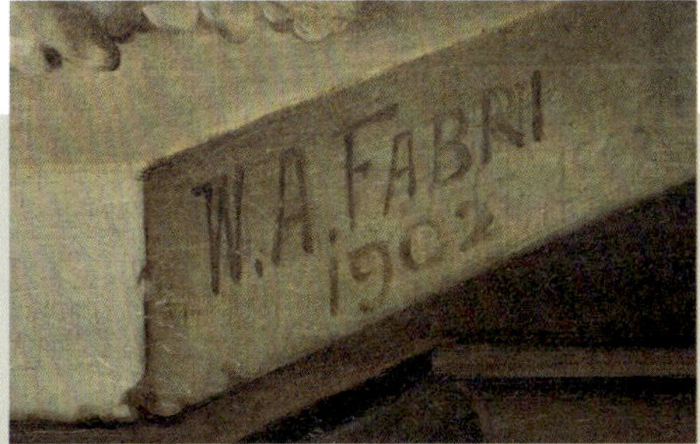

← The south wall with mythological figures and a view through to the Great Hall.
↑ The statue of the goddess Ceres painted on the south wall.
↗ Fabri signed the pedestal of the Diana statue.

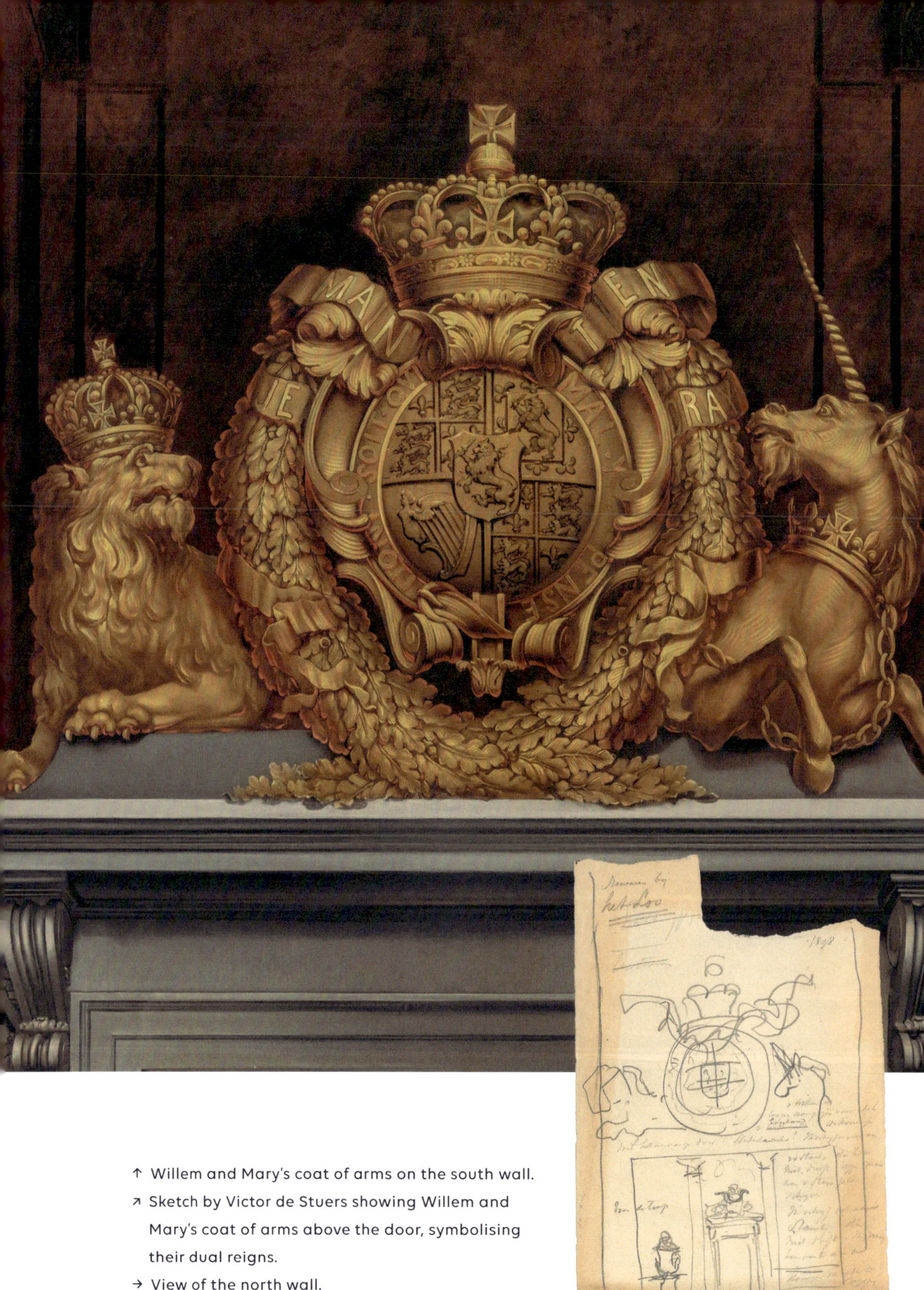

↑ Willem and Mary's coat of arms on the south wall.

↗ Sketch by Victor de Stuers showing Willem and Mary's coat of arms above the door, symbolising their dual reigns.

→ View of the north wall.

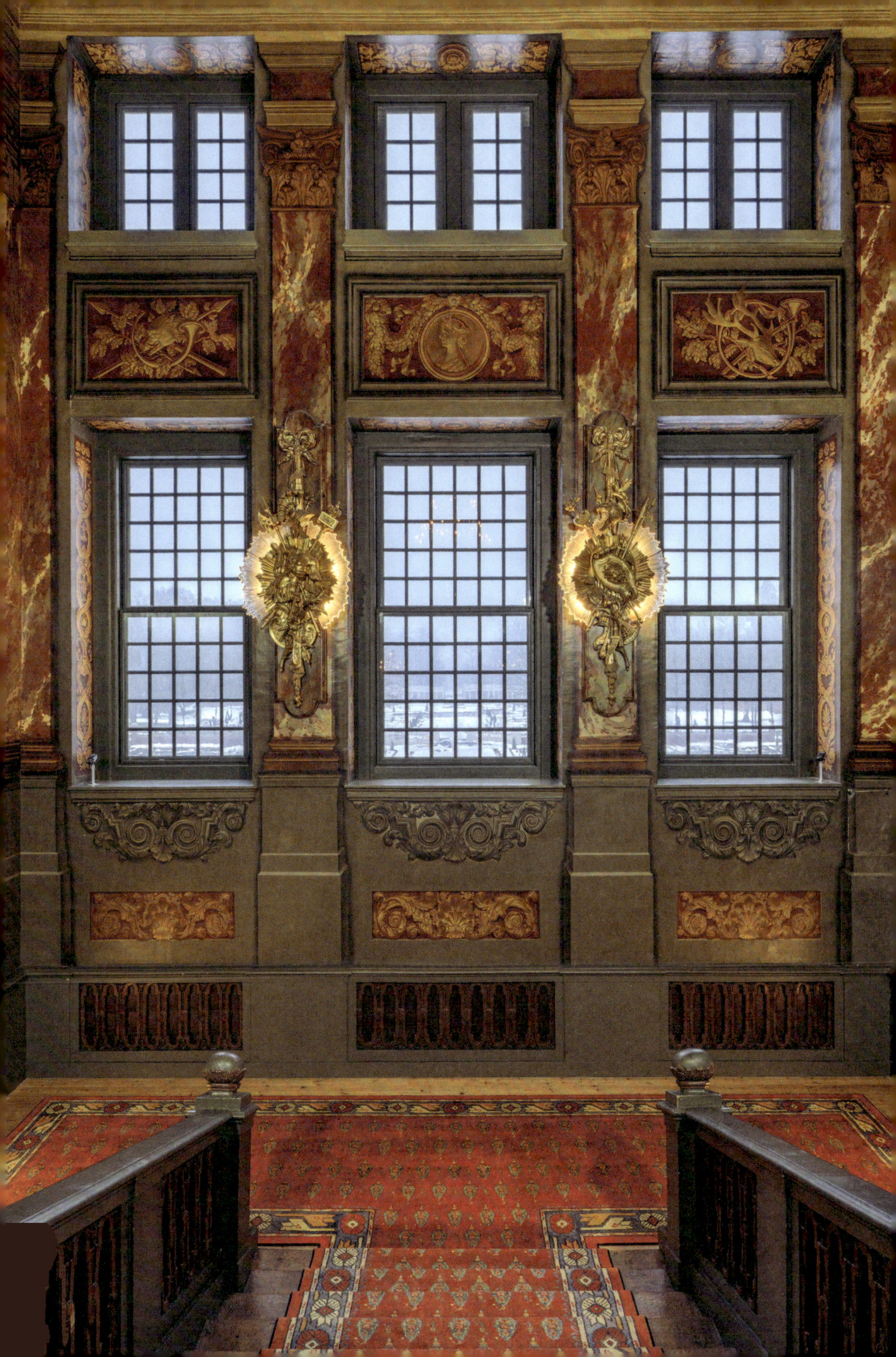

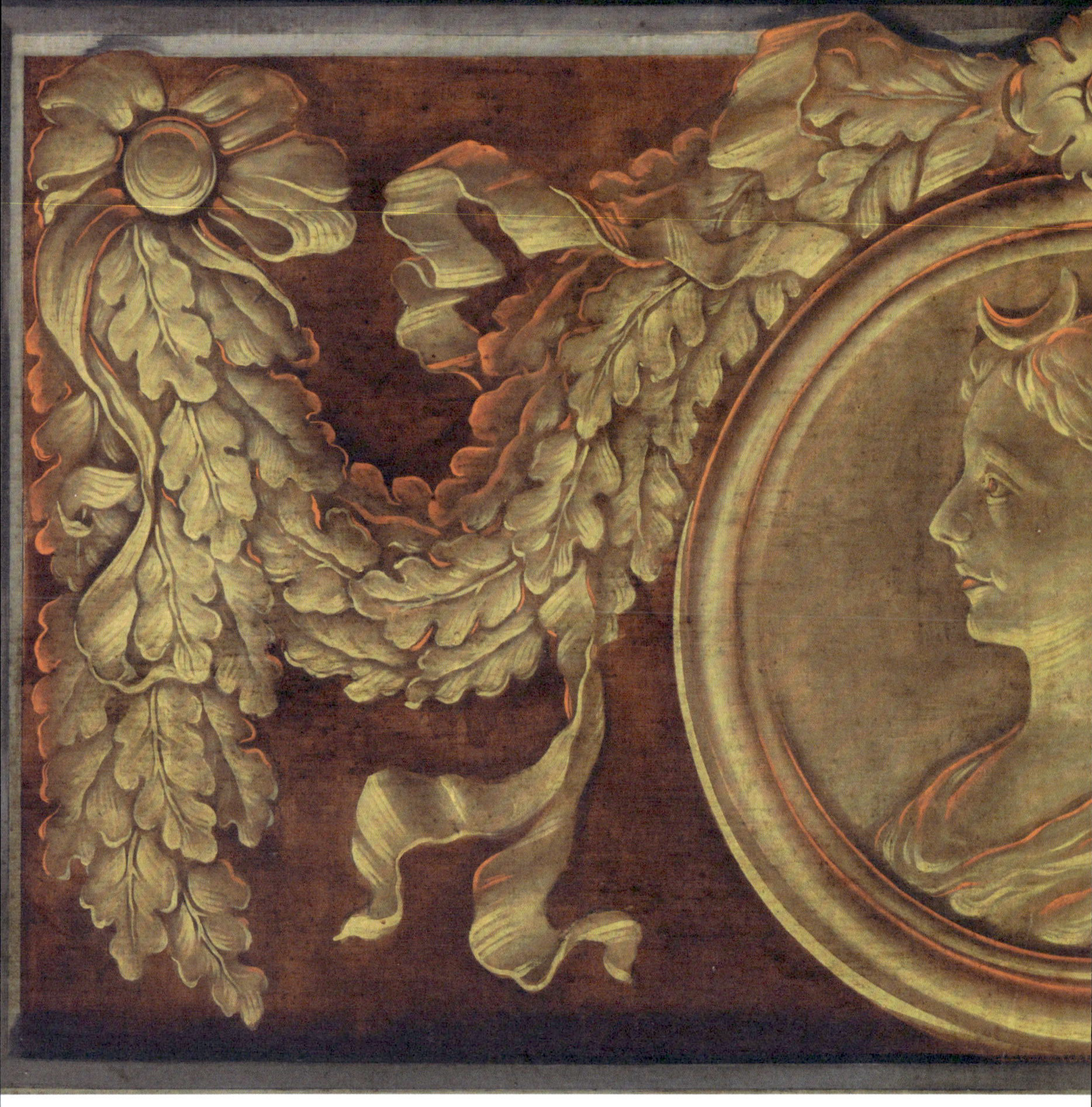

The medallion on the north wall featuring Queen Wilhelmina as Diana, Roman goddess of the hunt.

The north wall thus became an ode to Wilhelmina, who restored the staircase to its 17th-century glory. Her medallion hangs directly opposite the coat of arms of Willem and Mary on the south wall, equating her role in history with that of the king-stadtholder. All of these adaptations to the original show that in circa 1900 the mural was regarded mainly as decoration, with little or no political significance. The restoration team sought to honour Marot, but also took the opportunity to update the composition.

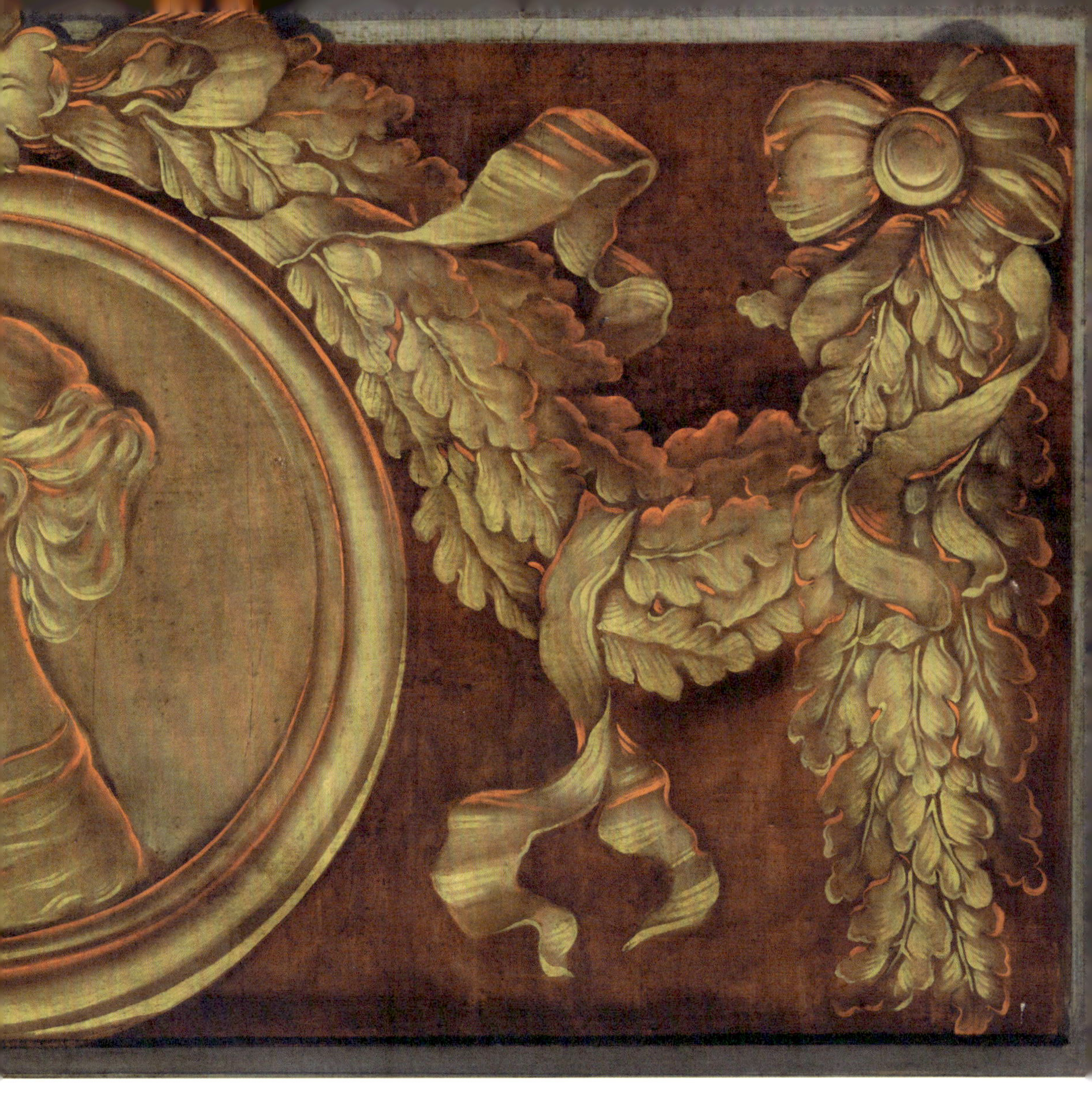

The reconstructed landscapes and architecture seem to be largely the work of Fabri's assistants, as their signatures appear only in these sections. Deviations from Marot's design came about as gaps in the image were filled, and through improvisation and the addition of extra details that provided depth and made the staircase feel more spacious.

To protect the painting from external influences and to enhance the sense of depth, Fabri applied a varnish to the paint layer. Nowadays varnishes are colourless, but in the early 20th century a pigment was sometimes added, to give the painting a light-yellow glow and make it appear older than it actually was. The result was entirely to the satisfaction of the queen and the painter himself. However, several years after completion, without Fabri's knowledge, new layers of varnish were applied. He discovered this when he came to see the painting around 1910. He was angry and informed the intendant, Joan A. van Steijn that he would no longer take responsibility for the quality of his work as previously guaranteed. In 1946, Fabri's assistants H.G. Luitwieler and K. Hoogendorp reported that, thanks to the varnish, the canvases were in a good state of preservation, though they found the sheen disruptive. If it were to be reduced, the effect would be gentler on the eye and the mural would work better. Whether the painting was indeed treated in accordance with their recommendations is uncertain.

Fabri's text on the first landing.

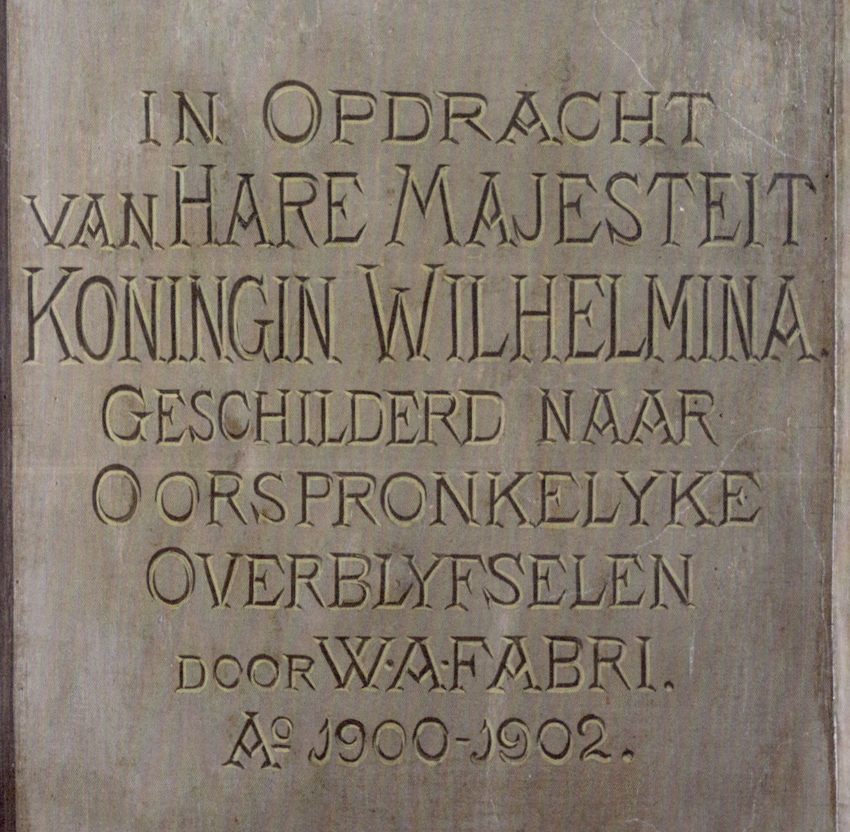

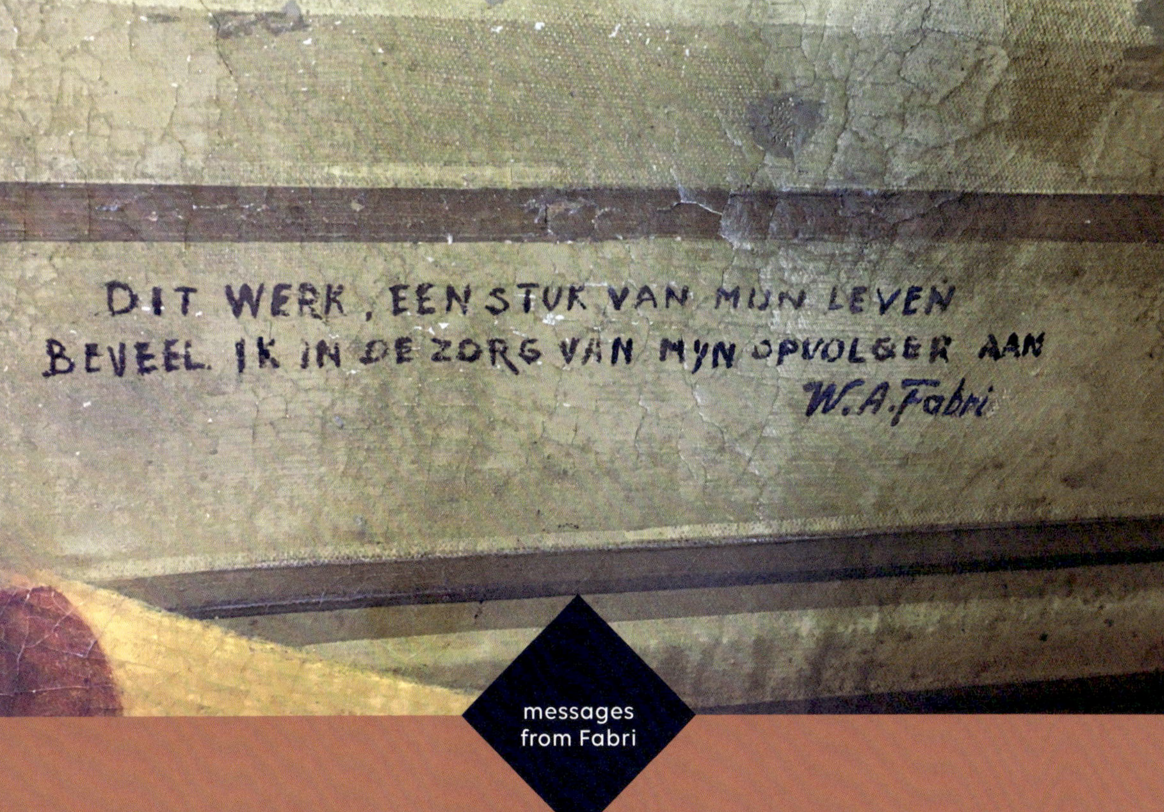

messages from Fabri

Willem Fabri must have been proud of his work on the Grand Staircase. He signed the painting in several places. The most prominent and expansive signature is in the righthand corner on the first landing: 'Painted after the original remains by W.A. Fabri. A[nn]o 1900-1902 on the orders of Her Majesty Queen Wilhelmina.' He also placed his signature on the pedestal of the painted statue of Diana, as well as on the ceiling and one of the columns. High on the west wall, in a spot not visible to visitors, Fabri left a message for future restorers: 'This work, part of my life, I leave to the care of my successor.'

↑ Fabri's message to his successors can only be seen from scaffolding.

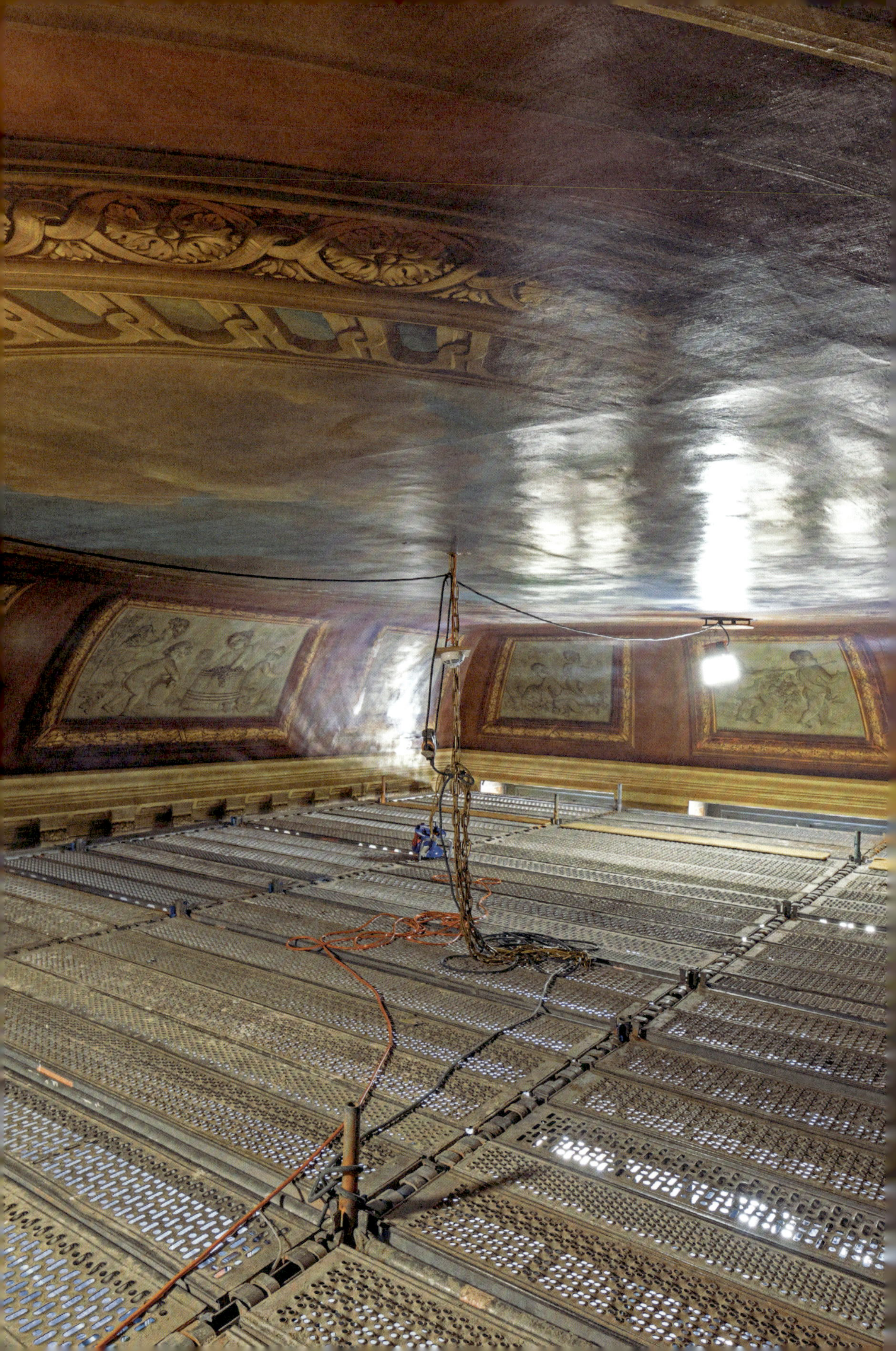

Unique Heritage

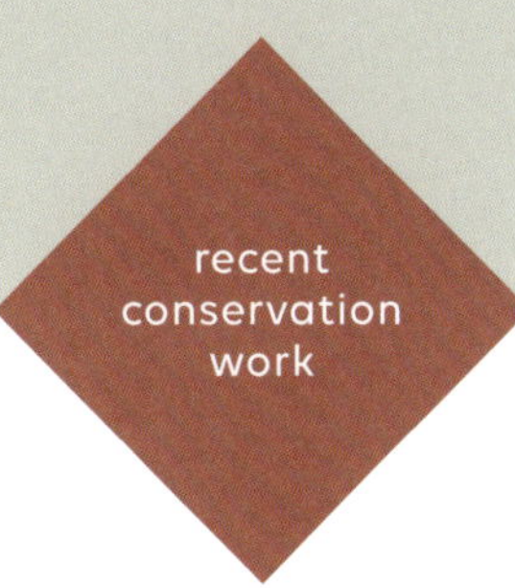

Wilhelmina's granddaughter Princess Margriet and her family were the last people to live at Paleis Het Loo. When they left in 1975 the palace was restored and converted into a national museum. This included work on the staircase. The paintings had once again sustained considerable damage over the course of the 20th century due to leaks and unstable climatic conditions. To prevent further deterioration, the staircase was sealed off from the open air from 1977 to 1980. This caused a significant rise in humidity, however, with serious implications including cracked plasterwork, flaking paint and mould.

Conservation by Jelle Otter

In 1980-1985 conservation work was performed by painter and conservator Jelle Otter (1925-2012) and his team. The complexity of the problems made the job tricky, but the conservators were able to stabilise the paint layers. Again, the final step was to apply a layer of varnish. Whereas a natural varnish made of resin had always been used previously, other options were now available. The conservation team opted for a modern synthetic varnish, with the expectation that this would not become discoloured, unlike natural resin varnishes. This would make it easier to maintain the large painting.

← **The ceiling as seen from scaffolding during conservation work in 2020.**

↓ **Restoration work on the east wall in the 1980s (p. 90–91).**

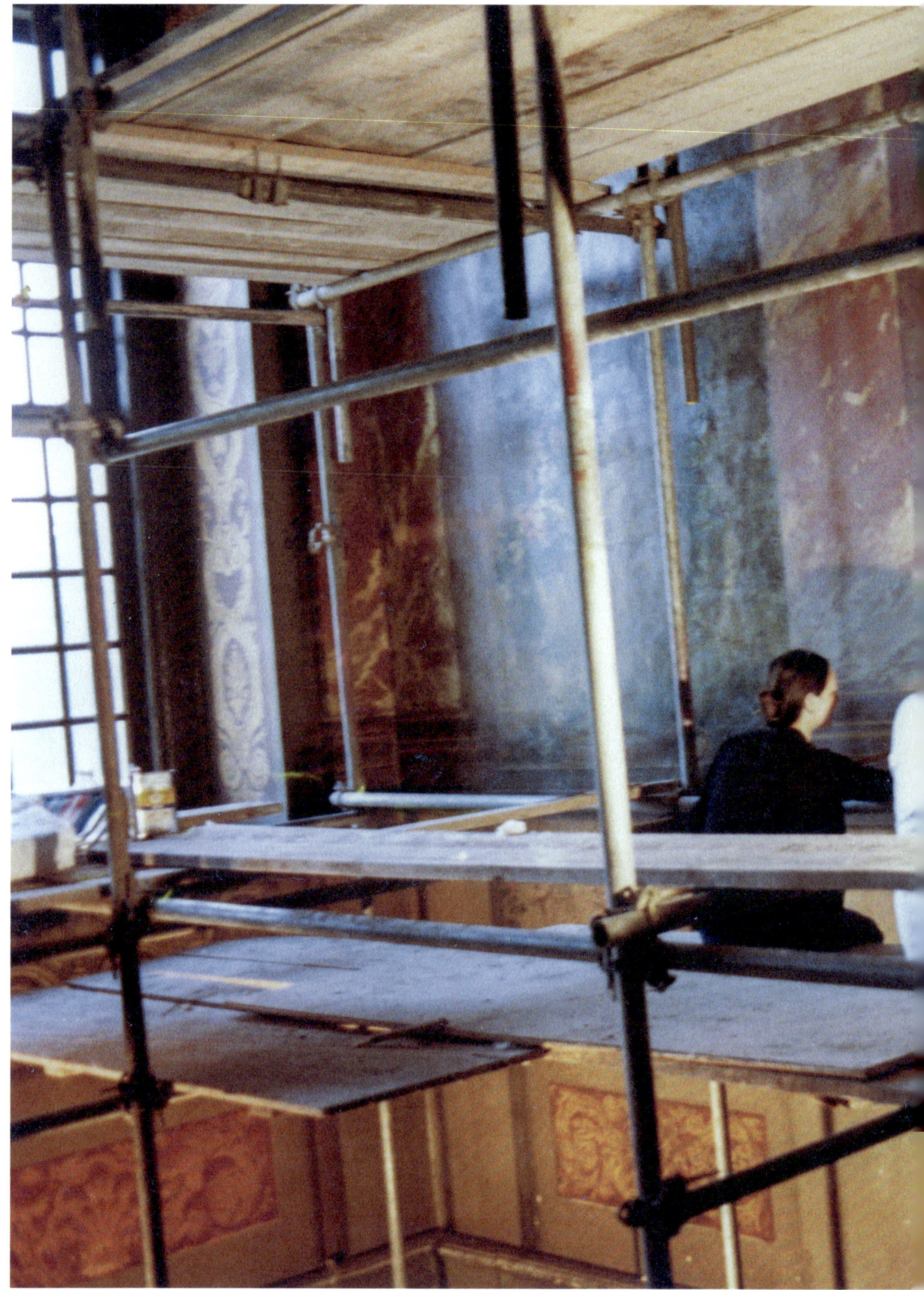

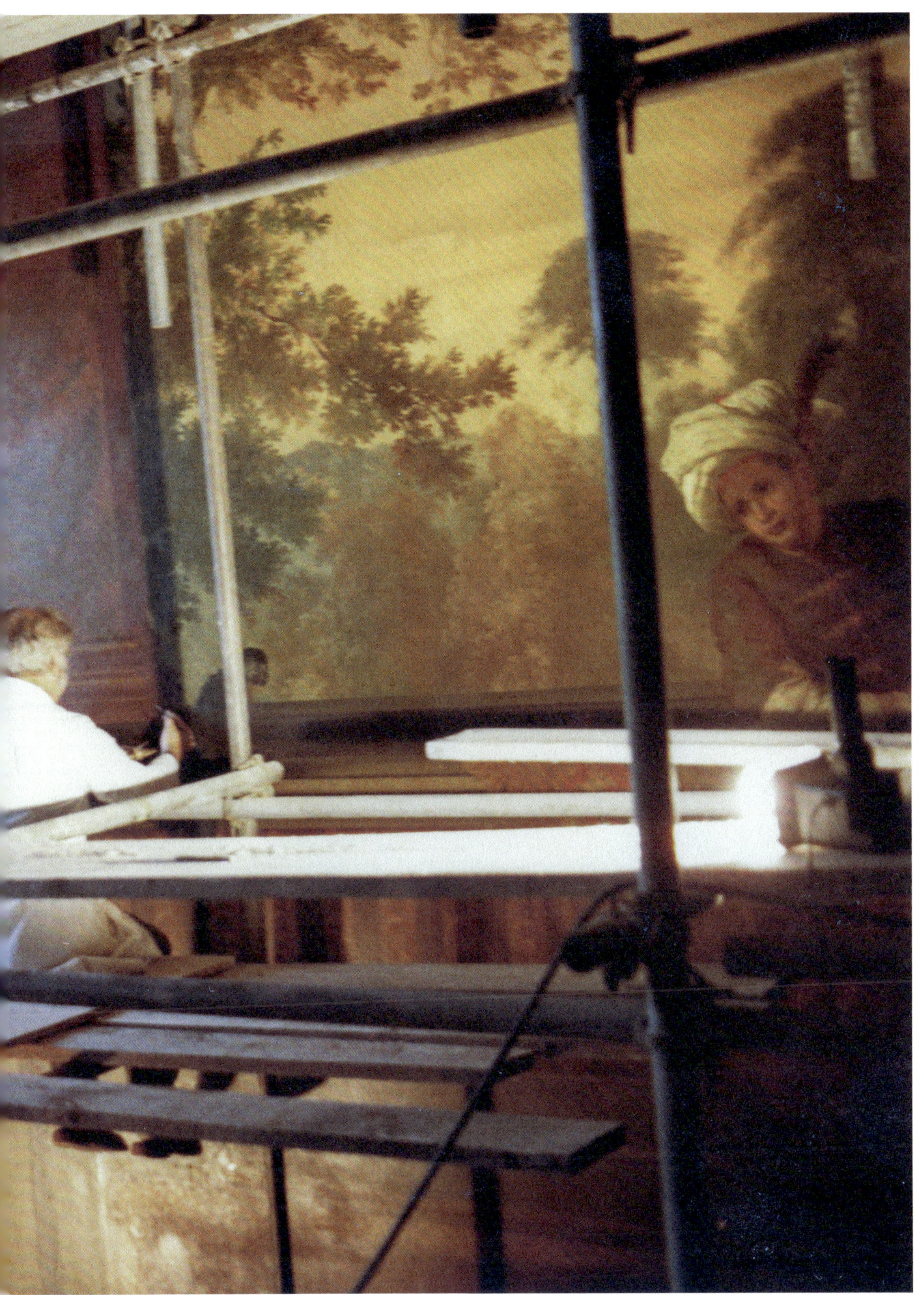

Preserved for posterity

The palace underwent further major restoration work from 2018 to 2022. The asbestos used as a fire retardant in the historic building in the 1980s had to be removed. An underground extension was also added to the museum. The condition of all collection items at the museum was meticulously assessed during this period.

In 2020, conservators from conservation institute SRAL found new problems with the painting on the staircase. The synthetic varnish from the 1980s had begun to bond with the underlying paint layer, a process that could eventually lead to irreparable damage. Work was again needed on the monumental painting. It was decided that the varnish layer should be removed and a more stable varnish applied. The conservators also treated the ceiling.

This round of conservation work entered its second phase in 2026. Work is now being carried out on the side walls, in full view of visitors this time. We are thus ensuring that a painting with a long history and unique heritage value remains preserved for future generations, so people can continue to stand on the stairs and touch the banister to connect for a moment with all the residents and visitors who have ever passed this way.

→ Now hundreds of years old, the staircase connects the 17th century with the present.

↓ A conservator removing the varnish from the ceiling in summer 2020 (p. 94-94).

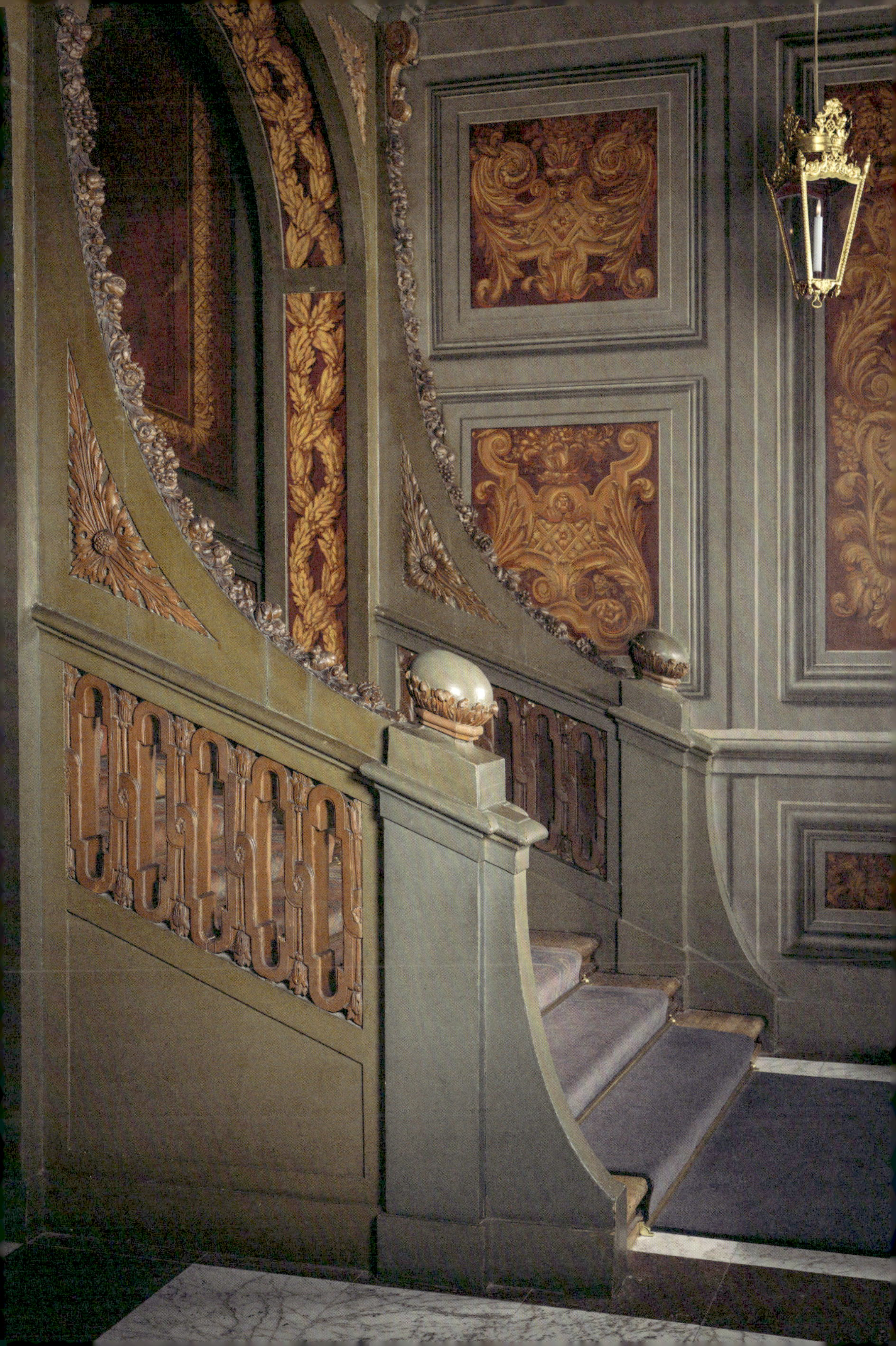

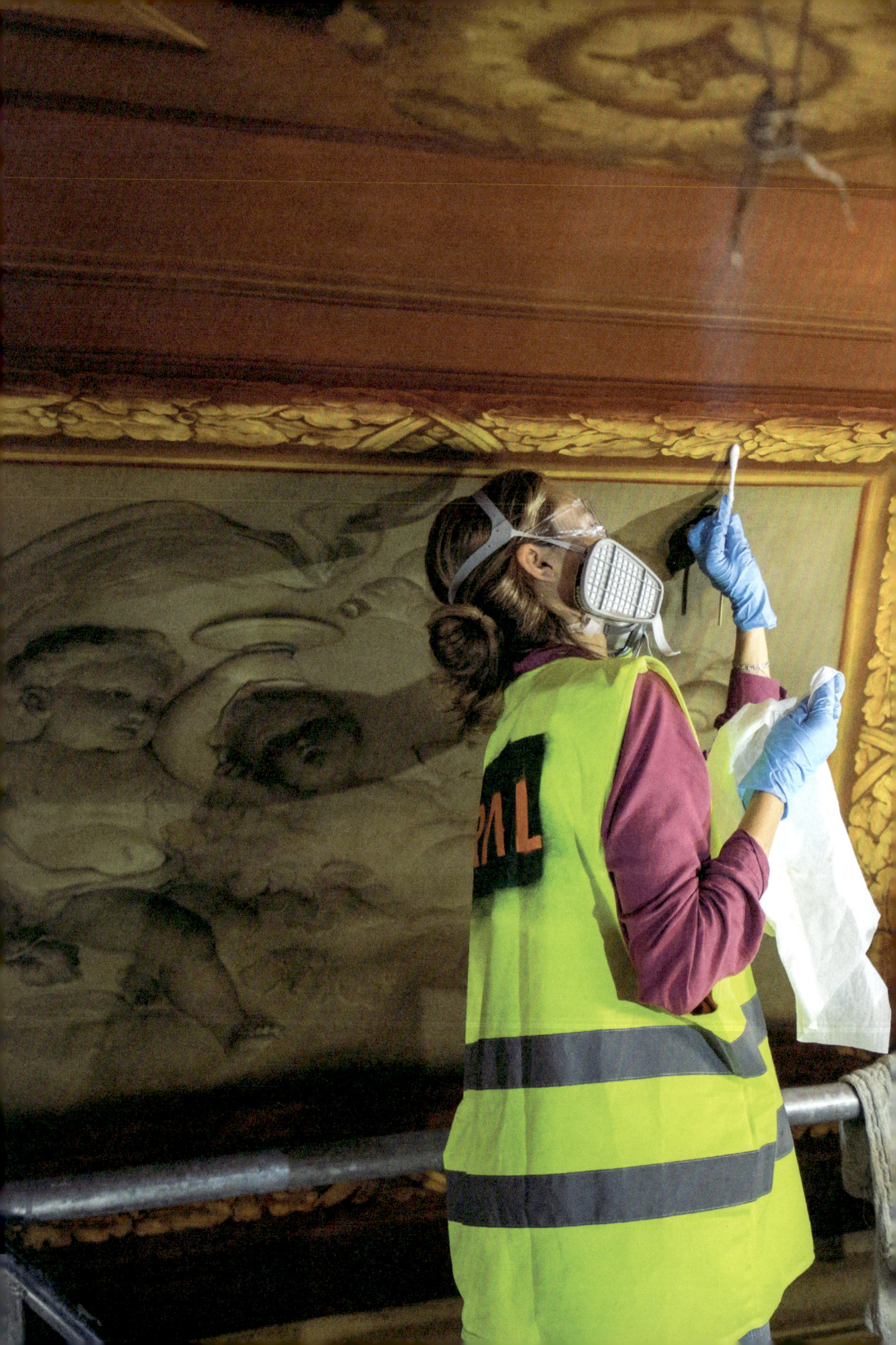